THIS IS THE
CHURCH...

THIS IS THE
CHURCH...

THE FIRST "SEASON" OF
OUR FATHER'S EVANGELICAL CHURCH

BRAD BROWN

For information about this title or to order other books and/or electronic media, contact the publisher:

Brad A Brown
bradbrownauthor.com
BRADSLAND@aol.com

ISBNs:
979-8-9870461-0-4 (hardcover)
979-8-9870461-1-1 (softcover)
979-8-9870461-2-8 (eBook)

Printed in the United States of America

Cover and Interior design: 1106 Design

This book is dedicated to

Doris Minkler
Norm Kusche
John and Judy Warren
Thank you for telling me
again, and again, and again,
of the old, old stories . . .

Brad Brown
Burbank, California
2002

ACKNOWLEDGMENTS

I would like to thank first and foremost, Dr. Brian Morrison, who, after reading only 15 pages of my primitive rough draft, prodded me with enough encouragement to forge ahead with my first novel.

Secondly, I deeply appreciate the dear friends who were willing to read the completed novel as a manuscript, chief among whom would be Marc Whitmore at Oxford Entertainment. It is solely upon the basis of their comments and compliments that my idea has been propelled into book form.

To my incredible wife, Cindy, and my wonderful daughters, Charissa and Courteney—my beloved family. Thank you for providing the loving foundation from which I could realize my dream. You gracefully endured the three-month-long ordeal of my writing, during which I was plagued with a good dose of mental isolation and preoccupation.

And lastly, to children and adult Sunday school teachers everywhere, past, present, and future. May this book be a distinct, resounding clap among the applause from heaven.

— Brad Brown
Burbank, California
2002

TABLE OF CONTENTS

PREFACE

The book you are about to read is very unique. In all my years of avid reading and habitual book-browsing, there is nothing quite like *This Is The Church* . . . or its three sequels. To be sure, some previous works have informed the series, like Charles Sheldon's 1896 classic, *In His Steps,* and the more recent *At Home in Mitford* series, by Jan Karen, written 100 years later. There was even an off-beat, 1978 novel that was required reading in college called *The Last Year of the War,* by Shirley Nelson, that had a part in lighting my book-writing fuse. These three prime examples are culled from the hundreds of influential books of many genres, shapes, and sizes that I have devoured over the decades.

But what makes *This Is The Church* . . . unique is that it could also be known by an alias, *This Is My Story* . . . In short, this book might be classified as a "fictional memoir," with the main character, Ian Block, acting as my first-person alter-ego. He moves and breathes in the fictional town of Monument, California, and is surrounded by a colorful cast of characters, most of whom also call Our Father's Evangelical Church their church home. Fact and fiction co-exist seamlessly in this hybrid as a template through which I can weave my own life and times. As such, the loom is full of fanciful liberties. Not everything you read actually happened, but much of it did. Truth is frequently stranger than fiction, both secular and sacred.

Each "season" of "Our Father's Evangelical Church" is deliberately structured differently. In *This Is The Church* . . . the textual shape and form follows the old English folk-rhyme, or "hand-rhyme" of the same name. Within its stanzas, Ian Block recalls adventures found in his first 40 years of life, especially life in the church.

Finally, a friendly reminder: At times Ian Block uses a rather fulsome vocabulary. Hence, these chronicles of Monument can include picturesque words like *sycophants*—which jumpstarts the whole narrative; *labyrinthine*—full of surprises and course corrections; *megalomaniacal*—when movers and shakers do just that, and the highfalutin *sesquipedalian*—which is just a big word describing those who use them! A totable dictionary could be a welcome co-companion with which to curl up by the proverbial fire. But consider the effort a worthy one, as word choices and their meanings reveal much about the user, hopefully making every encounter with these three-dollar words worth the price of admission!

With that, I hope you enjoy the first "season" of Our Father's Evangelical Church.

—Brad Brown, 2022

"This is my story,
This is my song"

—FANNY J. CROSBY

INTRODUCTION

"A little sleep, a little slumber,"

—PROVERBS 6:10A

"Sycophants!"

(One of my grandfather's favorite words—I had to look it up). "If I hear one more time 'That's how we have always done it,' heads are gonna roll!"

T hat was the beginning of the end! My grandfather, Deacon Colby Block, unleashed this final diatribe upon his alarmed lay-leader companions at Our Father's Evangelical Church in Monument, California. His opinion had something to do with a financial debacle, likely the result of procedural rote that had aligned itself with the Church's antiquated bylaws like a boa constrictor around an unsuspecting deer.

Some 50 years ago, he stormed out of this now-infamous deacon meeting and never set foot in *the* church or *a* church again! "Heads are gonna roll!" became one of my grandfather's most famous phrases, the veneration perpetuated by him saying it frequently.

"I will not be a party to a dishonest misrepresentation of money!" he had stated. Colby Block was the self-appointed spokesperson for the innocent, albeit naive, contributing members within Our Father's flock. His integrity was the bulwark of his earthly existence, and no amount of leadership aura would entice him to tarnish it. He remained silently "neutral" to his immediate family's subsequent dabbling in all things "church."

But he himself would never again risk his own association with an institution that might tarnish his sterling civic reputation.

Since that fateful night when "deacon heads rolled," his personal portrayal of the nuts and bolts of this now-legendary defection were cryptic at best. When asked, Colby Block steadfastly refused to divulge any of the particulars, participants, or breaches of protocol that rocked the house of God that night.

Nor did the friction ever find its way into the official minutes of the deacon meeting. The "gory details" were either strategically omitted or whitewashed altogether. The extent of the reckless, secretarial abandon and literary license was such that any fellow deacon reading the newfangled minutes from that night would have had to physically look up from the page in order to notice that my grandfather was actually missing! His chair at the Deacon Board table now glaringly empty.

And, miraculously, no unseemly culpability was ever levied against the elected church leadership by the money-giving flock at the time.

However, as a result of my grandfather "shaking the dust off his gospel of peace shoes" and never looking back over his shoulder, he carved himself an edifice of unanimous opinion embraced by all the population of Monument—whether secular or sacred, hierarchy or denizens—that Colby Block was indeed a man of *honesty!*

The stories that have posthumously filtered down through the years of his integrity and acts of heroic service within the community—to friends, strangers, business associates, or pestering clients—have truly bolstered me. It has been such an arsenal of "heads will roll" model fuel. I constantly feel his eyes boring down upon me as he whoops and hollers from the heavenly grandstands, along with that ethereal "cloud of witnesses" (perhaps to the great chagrin of the other prophets and biblical luminaries also populating the bleachers and rooting for other exasperated pilgrims), "Don't you ever sacrifice your integrity for . . . anything, Ian! Be honest at any cost!"

The deafening cheering imagined by those out-of-breath Hebrews (to which the "cloud of witnesses" analogy was originally offered), provided them stimulating spiritual sustenance in order for each of them to finish the proverbial race. My imagination finds equally sustaining stamina in the ear-splitting bravado of my grandfather as he pontificates over the din of that stadium in eternity. Shouting through cupped hands that he is proud of his grandson and promises to be a forefather's soundtrack of wisdom to propel me on my life's journey, or . . .

"Heads are gonna roll!"

"Call me Ian"—to borrow from the opening of Herman Melville's *Moby Dick*—Ian Block. I am the son of Seth and Nancy Block. And, yes, I have had that age-old adage mischievously applied to me on numerous occasions throughout my life that I am a "chip off the ole Block." *Which* Block is the question—my father or grandfather? I suppose that depends upon which Block one has had the pleasure of encountering. As I have stated, my grandfather has achieved posthumous legendary status in the community. My father has also endeavored to carry on the Block name in and around Monument. In response to the reverent churning of the Colby Block rumor mill, Seth Block has tried to carefully place one foot at a time into the now-cavernous, symbolic footsteps of his own, immortalized father. As such, Seth Block has been a consistent, hard-working, loving father, with only the seemingly magical erudition of the television fathers and pop psychologists of the 1950s as the standard bearers available for achieving successful domestication in raising myself and my brother, Owen. Even so, it might be unfairly perceived that my father does not possess the backbone of the great Colby Block—all because my father has *stayed* in the church and weathered many a storm of suspicion and controversy over the years, rather than create sensational news by storming out of all things ecclesiastical.

Determined not to take the easy way out by moving on before God moves in, Seth Block has remained steadfast throughout blistering seasons of pastoral transitions and its bedfellow, congregational upheavals and migrations (accompanied by cowardly backstabbing, gossip, and ridicule), all under the suspicious excuse of hearing "God calling" elsewhere.

"How they could be listening to God calling them is beyond me!"—I once secretly overheard my deflated, cynical father say to my mother after he had come home very late one night from yet another marathon deacon meeting, which were scheduled in rapid succession during these periods of rumblings.

"They never close their mouths long enough to *listen* to the Almighty as they are too busy heaving cannonballs of accusations and tabloid rumors over the walls of the church!"

This was the best he could do in rendering word pictures (the imagery was undoubtedly borrowed subconsciously from the head-tossing tucked into 2nd Samuel, Chapter 20, when a woman wise beyond her years flings the decapitated noggin of Sheba, a horn-blowing, bickering Benjamite, over the fence to be deftly caught by an appeased Commander Joab), as my father desperately attempted to communicate the spiritual warfare that had, yet again, in viciously reliable cycles, crashed down the door of our sleepy little church. This venom possesses both pulpit and pew. It seems so uncharacteristic of normally predictable, dependently bleating sheep.

But "evening wolves" (as the prophet Habakkuk described them), only *temporarily* disguise their numbers! At that common finale to any church's masquerade ball—the preacher switch— when all of the individual, spiritual façades are discarded, it is revealed that many have come with the same popular "sheep" costume of supposed gentleness and subservience. Yet underneath the fake-wool outfit sweats a cunning, lupine predator! Sadly, this turns out to be a maddeningly prevalent condition throughout the various sheep pens that make up the so-called "sanctuary"! The sheep suit is, in fact, the costume of choice for any wolf or wolves during a church transition. It is designed with seamless care by the one masquerading as an "angel of light." He inspects each thread and hem before allowing any duped believer to become a wolf wannabe by donning the mask, zipping up the back, and assuming the deceptive role of self-appointed "sheepherder."

However, when the church ball is over, and the deflected usurpers have been forced to migrate to another "call of the wild," there remains a genuinely loyal, weeded-out "remnant" of the original flock. Flock leftovers whose first task is to pick up the trash from the party, sweep the confetti, mop up the spilled puddles of punch, and sincerely forge ahead in unity as they follow a newly elected, "called of God" shepherd.

Suffice it to say, my father was one of those who "remained steadfast," a rather refreshing pronouncement of immovability and dedication in the face of numerous cycles of spiritual supply and demand on behalf of sheep suffering from an all-too-frequent "greener grass" malady!

As a son of a deacon, I, too, was destined to "stay put" through all the tempestuous seasons of Our Father's Evangelical Church of Monument, California, and personally experience the ebb and flow of life as it is absorbed through the filters of growing up in the church. I had the ubiquitous lexicon of Sunday schools written all over me. It was as if all of those quirky teachers (both gregarious and monotonous); the great Bible stories illustrated with colorfully robed, neatly trimmed bearded characters; the flannel boards populated with all the royalty and mental cases of Holy Writ; the somewhat forced arts and crafts to tie it all in; and the plastic swords festooned with construction-paper awards for short-term "storing up nuts for winter" memorization, were inculcated into my body, soul, and spirit by an unearthly transfusion of some profound curriculum for getting through life. To be sure, I was unable to recognize all of this as it went in. I became aware of its efficacy only when I later found myself in the dark trenches of life's snares and temptations. To my surprise, the cavalry that came to my rescue time and time again sported a banner reminiscent of the Crusades of old, emblazoned with the fiery letters "Mrs. Hawkins' Third Grade Sunday School Class."

Ironically, even though He had been the quintessential hero of all Sunday school classes for time immemorial, I was very uncomfortable with saying the name of "Christ" out loud. This stemmed from an event that occurred in our household when I was in the third grade. Back then, my mother and father resembled Henry and Alice Mitchell—the parents of "Dennis the Menace." My father was tall and lean, with a shock of neatly combed black hair; my mother was a moderately built, natural blonde. I seemingly inherited the combination platter: tall and lean, with dishwater-blond hair. My mother was poring over the family bills at the dining-room table. Her sour mood derived from intense consternation as she endeavored to strike a balance with the previous month's financial upheaval, spontaneity, and chaos.

So, she went sleuthing each month for that elusive amount of money that was not responding to the checkbook-entry roll call, which she performed in anticipation of all the correct amounts lining up dutifully, present and accounted for. My mother had very little tolerance for errant or delinquent entries and pursued the resultant M.I.A. money with undaunted resilience. This particular "hunting season" was taking place on a lazy Sunday afternoon. We had come home from church, eaten our Sunday lunch, and were enjoying a most coveted chunk of free time after our usual activity-laden week. The church service that morning had closed with a rousing hymn celebrating the propitiation of sins so perfectly implemented by the crucifixion of our Savior. As the music to the finale of the service was so forceful, my third-grade mind retained the catchy melody, and a smattering of the probably profound lyrics. On my way to the refrigerator to get an after-lunch snack, I walked by my search-and-seizure mother glowering over the checkbook at the dining-room table. I was allowing the fragments of the hymn sung hours before to provide the cadence to my stroll to the kitchen. As the words flitted about my brain, legitimate fragments would coalesce to validate my retention. Consequently, I leisurely sang out loud what little I could remember. Unfortunately, all that was left of one of the stanzas after my shoddy memory had finished sifting through it, was the word "Christ." As it was the only lyrical souvenir I possessed from a particular line of the hymn that was playing in my head, I half-blurted, half-sang out the one-word remnant of the third stanza of hymn# 465, "Christ!"

Since it was a rather brief oral contribution to the dead-quiet family air space, it was not perceived to have any semblance of melody attached to it. I had my back to my mother as I walked past her, and my insidious musical timing broke her concentration. All she heard was the exclamation of a proper noun that was anything but proper! She probably assumed that I had stubbed my toe or that my hand had got caught in the refrigerator door. Needless to say, she turned around and instantly lashed out at me, heedless of any explanation on my part, that I was to never, ever use *that* name again!

She was under the distinct impression that I had sworn.

This was completely out of character for me! I had been born and raised on those intimidating Ten Commandments, and was not about to be so brazen as to "use the Lord's name in vain"—number three. I was keenly aware of the high body count recorded in the Old Testament of not only those poor folks who misread or ignored the sacred Scriptures and would try to steady toppling arks of the covenants, but also those who tried to complain against a master of ceremonies, like Moses, and found themselves swallowed up by the jaws of Mother Earth! It was a verbal land mine that I would not risk! (My sixth-grade Sunday school classmates and I would later create a militant battle cry that we would affectionately whisper to each other when confronted with yet another grisly Bible story, "Torah, Torah, Torah!" Not only did it commemorate a star-studded World War II movie that was gracing local theaters at the time, but it was also our way of expressing, by the enhanced spelling, the S.O.S. so often recorded in the Scriptures as a result of the divine surprise attack that would sweep down like some cosmic firestorm, or seep through the walls and under doors like some hideous airborne disease on those poor, unsuspecting souls of the O.T. when they dared to violate any principle or precept tucked into the Pentateuch and ended up either doing spiritual K.P. or were D.O.A.) Even the New Testament had its lethal moments—like the terminal tithing of Ananias and Sapphira!

My mother offered no opportunity for rebuttal, and I was forced to sheepishly return to my room (without my snack!) and ruminate on the excoriating sentence pronounced upon me:

Ian Block: a user of the Lord's name in *vain!*

This brand, this verbal mark of the Beast, so absorbed at such a pliable, impressionable age, rendered me quite paranoid for decades to come in uttering the word "Christ" in any circumstance, no matter how legitimate or appropriate. It is sad to say that the nomenclature by which I had personally secured my hall pass up the stairway to heaven was now misconstrued as a "dirty word" in the erroneously exaggerated "scar files" of my memory. To this day, my mother does not know the tongue-lashed damage she had wrought on that fateful Sunday afternoon. She had looked up from the checkbook and concluded something totally false about the oral behavior of her very reverent child, rendering him not more reverent, but less, by my reticence to further an intimate relationship with One whose name I couldn't even utter properly. How could I ever sidle up to the mighty Son of God when He supposedly insisted on remaining standoffish and punitive when I wrongly called out His name?

Fortunately, Jesus—who loves me, this I know—made it a point to carefully distinguish for me between what is respectful and what had originally evoked misplaced holy terror as a youth. He has sought to eradicate anything and everything that might potentially impede our intimacy over the years—as the Bible tells me so.

In spite of this one misunderstanding about what constitutes "swearing," my mother was otherwise well-intentioned in most all respects, and diligently endeavored to lovingly introduce the author of the Bible to me every night prior to my going to sleep. I remember, from my earliest bedtime experiences, my mother simplistically explaining to me the eclectic, innermost parts of the Body of Christ with a well-worn little English folk-rhyme with verses that were accompanied by the most fascinating, seemingly complicated movements of the hand and fingers synchronized to each phrase. She would begin by stating

"This is the church . . . "

She would then fuse her hands into one fist with inward, interlocking fingers, the two upright thumbs formed what looked like welcoming double-doors.

"This is the steeple."

Her "pointer fingers" on both hands would shoot up and lean against each other, replicating a steeple at the front end of my mother's house of God of compressed hands.

"Open the door,"

—she would then separate her hands at her wrists and spread them. This would reveal the interlocked fingers underneath . . .

"and there's all the people!"

—she would wiggle her fingers at this proclamation, just as if the fingers had heard their collective cue and began to mill about within the hallowed halls of her palms.

The second verse, although not nearly as common throughout memorable, singsong verses of childhood, had fascinating visuals to accompany the prose.

"This is the parson . . .
going upstairs."

—at that, my mother would release the fingers of her interlocked hands, save for her two little fingers. She would then miraculously pivot the interlocked "pinkies" and twist one of her hands around so that she could begin to interlock the remaining fingers, in sequence, backwards, up the front of the hand facing me. As she progressed, it gave the illusion of someone going up a flight of stairs! But the trickiest part was yet to come:

"He's in his pulpit . . .
saying his prayers!"

—her hands were now interlocked, knuckles to knuckles, by her four fingers (her thumbs were dangling freely), she then twisted both wrists in unison toward her, and her hands amazingly formed a lectern of fingers resembling a pulpit! The thumb of her left hand had mysteriously been incorporated into the top layer of the finger-woven "pulpit," leaving her right thumb free to move about on top of the pulpit, bending and genuflecting in an expression of bowed penitence.

The first time I saw this literal sleight of hand performed by mother, my eyes had widened in abject fascination at the uncanny way she had maneuvered her arms, palms, and fingers to re-create both parishioner and parson in a three-dimensional illustration of the verse she was reciting.

She would perform this ritual even long after I was supposedly too old for it.

After prayers, my mother kissed me good night and quietly slipped out of my bedroom (gently massaging her fingers as she went against the imminent onslaught of a pre-arthritic condition that had befallen them as a result of their brief show-and-tell performance moments before). I lay me down to sleep and began to contemplate, in childlike perplexity, accompanied by great cognitive friction, just *who* my mother had meant when she announced, "There's all the people!"

My mental wanderings traveled with intense consternation, and I pondered over and over again,

"There's all the people"? "There's all the people"?

Even now as an adult, I can still picture those interlocking fingers of my mother's all wiggling with distinct individuality, yet still in strange, rhythmic unison as orchestrated by her invitation of the verse and wonder anew,

"There's all the people? . . ." "the people? . . ."

By "the people," she couldn't possibly mean the autocratic, dictatorial political monster who usurps the throne of some unsuspecting country and begins to annihilate all of those underlings who did not first abide by his coup when it was in progress. He particularly homes in on those "religious ones" who found his upward-ladder-ascension not only highly aggressive, but antagonistic to their collective faith as well. This potentate continues on his murderous spree until he is finally overthrown, finding himself in exile only to be confronted and comforted by the very faith he sought to obliterate. In his desperation and seclusion, he bends the ear of God and is heard.

By "the people," she couldn't possibly mean the quiet, unsuspecting loner, who is nefariously connected with the disappearances of many innocent spontaneous acquaintances. After some extensive investigation, his apartment is found to be littered with the final traces of his victims. He is discovered to have engaged in an unspeakably violent behavior—only associated in *modern* society with disastrous plights of isolation and desperation, or the rituals of some long-forgotten tribe safely secluded on earthly terrain rarely frequented by the "civilized"—cannibalism! Moments before his execution, he is counseled by a man of faith and is invited into a heavenly eternity.

She couldn't possibly mean the abusive single mother who, induced by alcohol, verbally berates her children and physically batters them. She deems this necessary in order to secure a nebulous concept of discipline out of respect for her as a parent that has long since disappeared.

She couldn't possibly mean that businessman whose alter ego of the wholesome "family man" he portrays at church is really a voracious consumer of child pornography wherever he can graze. His appetite is particularly appeased in the privacy of some hotel room out of town under the guise of a "business trip." Upon discovery by a co-worker, the pedophile repents to his family and congregation and begins to trudge up the mountain of pain and shame he built for himself in an effort to reach the summit of a restored reputation and a resuscitated integrity.

By "the people," she couldn't possibly mean that grizzled, sleeping mendicant I had to suddenly step over in the park who was writhing in a cocoon of malnutrition and drugs as I made my way to the outdoor birthday party of my best friend at the time.

Or the lady with the big blue hair who sang all of the solos during the Sunday morning choir anthem at church, who would like nothing better than to garner a six-figure salary as a musical celebrity and who saw this Christian gig as a mere steppingstone to getting there.

She couldn't possibly mean the youth pastor who swears on numerous occasions in conversation strictly for emphasis, or so he says. He confesses to a hearkening back to those glorious pre-conversion days when he had freedom of vocabulary.

Or the burly individual I had the privilege of sitting next to at the crowded local theater who was wearing only a tank top T-shirt and sported the rankest case of pungent body odor to have ever explored my nasal passages!

By "the people," she couldn't possibly have meant the boy who was carving his initials and those of his girlfriend with his pocket knife into the back of the wooden pew right before my very eyes during Vacation Bible School.

Or the girl with the long, blond hair who sat directly in front of me at school. She would constantly tip her head back and flip her golden tresses conceitedly onto my desk, obliterating everything on its surface.

Or the boy who threatened to beat me up for no apparent reason and then subsequently gathered his friends to pummel me with kickballs after school.

Or the teller with one arm at the bank who constantly sniffs during transactions.

Or that mean clerk at the video store with his two front teeth missing who glares at me.

Or the little girl with the one roaming eye.

By "the people" she couldn't possibly mean . . .

She didn't,

but *He* did.

PART ONE

CHAPTER ONE

THIS IS THE CHURCH . . .

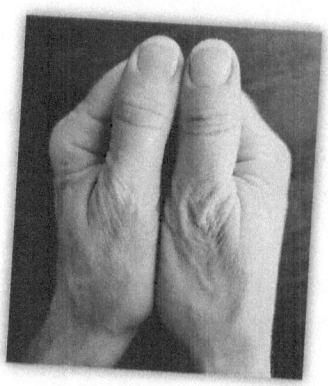

Yes, indeed, this is the church: part hospital—part armory, part old-folks' home—part nursery, part academy—part mental ward, part beacon—part neighborhood irritant, part gathering place—part evil deterrent, part historical land-mark—part modern convenience, part infirmary—part insane asylum, part saint—part sinner, part divine—part dementia, part charismatic—part criminal, part professor—part lunatic, part opulent—part destitute, yet, somehow, by some enigmatic heavenly adhesive, whole!

This divine invention was the home of my first introduction to the Savior (and my woefully tardy but eventually obedient baptism!), my first kiss, my first girlfriend, and my first "ministry opportunity." When functioning properly, this institution, affec-tionately known as the "Body," has been so carefully constructed that it can potentially embrace all of the triumphs of a life and, at the same time, withstand all of the tragedies of that same life with uncanny ability and spiritual savviness.

Like the flippers that guard the bottom of a pinball machine, you shoot through life with speed and agility, racing back and forth and slamming into "bumpers" that cause all sorts of internal and external bells to go off, racking up point victories when the correct trajectory is achieved. Yet to prevent you from careening out of sight and out of the "game," the flippers are positioned to push you back into the race just in the nick of time as you begin to bottom out! One's ball free-falling past the flippers of the church is either by unfortunate circumstances or sheer determination, requiring specific self-destructive aiming in order to do so. Or, worse still, the church itself is caught by surprise asleep at the buttons as their charges fall through the crack caused by their collective irresponsibility. I, for one, am grateful for the life perspective, the oft-denounced boundaries, and the occasional catapult Our Father's Evangelical Church provided me so that I could stay "on the ball" and not be swallowed up by the gravitational pull of a ball-swallowing world!

Our church was situated on a remarkable piece of real estate at the base of the Sierra Nevada foothills of Monument, California (this spur of the mountain chain would later be named more specifically "San Gabriel"). Monument was originally called "Vista Pacifica" by the settling Spaniards of the 1700s to commemorate the spectacular view of the pristine Pacific Ocean afforded by many of the promontories at the time within the prime acreage that would eventually become the township of Monument in 1927. Our church commands just such a view, although the breathtaking panorama has now been relegated to only occasional days when the air quality permits beholding such an historic vista.

The church was built some 60–70 years ago in a neighborhood nestled at the base of the "monument" after which the town was named, or re-named. As the terrain and foothills are predominantly composed of granite, it was the dream of 39-year-old Max Stellar of Grand Rapids, Michigan, when he came out to California in the 1920s, as an architect for the rich and famous, to literally carve a name for himself against the backdrop of our picturesque little hamlet. As the story goes, Stellar had been inspired by a recent summer excursion to South Dakota, and profoundly affected by not only the power and majesty of Mount Rushmore, but also by the miracle of sculpting that was reflected in the four confident presidential heads that remained facially austere and even defiant against the seemingly insurmountable odds that nature had and would fling at them. Max came back home to California and immediately purchased some 15 to 20 predominantly vertical acres going up the cliff face of the Sierra Nevada foothills of "Vista Pacifica" that were untouched by human hands. He set out to sculpt (in his spare time from making those studio-contracted movie stars of old a little more comfortable in their living spaces) the head of his favorite movie star, Rudolph Valentino, in full Arab headdress, as depicted in the 1921 classic movie, *The Sheik*. With a crew that fluctuated between 10 and 15 fellow architects, movie makers, demolition experts, artists, naturalists, and sculptors, Max worked for many years at carving the 100-foot face of his beloved movie star permanently into the Southern California topography. Interestingly, Max and his crew strictly worked from left to right, as it was somehow advantageous to the sculpting process—the result of the slope of the sheer cliff, the downhill pattern of the massive amounts of falling chiseled debris, the flow of rainwater, and its resultant erosion of growth and topsoils during inclement seasons.

Amidst all of the excitement generated by this artistic defacing of the landscape was the uncharacteristically flexible "Vista Pacifica" City Council. At the time, the Council consisted of only a handful of citizens who had built homes in the area. They also worked in some capacity, either in Hollywood proper (some 25 miles to the west) or in other local industries that were continuously cropping up. Others had cultivated farmland still replete in the sparsely populated San Fernando Valley. Together they decided to re-name the town, in the haughty heat of the moment, to "Monument."

Ironically, it seemed, just as soon as the name was officially adopted, the civic ceremonies all completed, and Monument legally recorded as a city in the State of California in 1927, Max Stellar died of a sudden heart attack in the fifth year of his Rudolph Valentino project. Having left no specific prodigy to finish the project (he was single and had no children to carry on his name or career), his other co-workers slowly lost interest at varying stages for other obligations and endeavors clamoring for their attentions. Thus, the left half of the 100-foot face of Rudolph Valentino—a left ear, left eye, whole nose, and half heroically smiling lips—was abandoned to the inquisitive, destructive, tenacious exploration of nature.

The hillside brush that surrounded "The Sheik" began to prey upon it, and the indigenous animal life sought to inhabit it (like the family of raccoons that currently call Rudolph's left nostril "home"). In addition to abruptly encroaching upon the rugged yet serene backdrop of the city, the cloven project has also permanently chiseled into the psyche of the perplexed inhabitants of Monument a gigantic "to do" list in the sky! Not to be outdone by all of the attention drawn to Monument, a High School in downtown Hollywood adopted the Valentino "Sheik" as their mascot as well!

Of course, the unfinished half-head of Rudolph has fostered as many rib-poking jokes and barbs over the years as my last name. Virtually every Christmas, against all of the imposed city ordinances, some prankster-vandal, under the erroneous pretense of creative originality, climbs up the partial face of Rudolph and spray-paints his nose red. After so many years of defacing in December and corrective sandblasting in January, the nose now retains a year-round red hue!

Even Our Father's Evangelical Church was not immune to fostering its own series of jokes and quips over the years regarding the 100-foot partial sculpture that looked down on the church property from a height of 50 feet (where the chin begins). Many of the remarks were jocular derivations from our very own hymnals! Classic phrases such as "Our sacred [half] head," "His eyes [eye] are [is] on the sparrow," and "He hides me in the [partial] cleft of the rock" did not escape a double meaning unique to our church and caused a smirk or two. Church members were compelled to admit that, on the occasions when they sang these verses, their minds were engaged in a shameful worshipful duality. They would try, in vain, to pensively focus singularly on the Godhead, but find themselves pursing their lips in a worthless attempt to deflect the devious smile that was imminently forming at the corners of their mouth, caused by a mental picture of Rudolph staring down at them from outside the stained-glass windows, which defiantly replaced their intended holy thoughts with comparative hilarity.

Valentino Avenue is one of only two off-ramps from the freeway that take you up the hill and drop you into the heart of downtown

Monument (the other being the highly unoriginal Main Street, which runs perpendicular to Valentino, bisecting the avenue about halfway up the hill). Since the town is built on this incline that ascends toward the foothills, the freeway commands an excellent view of the half-head of Rudolph beyond. Even in its unfinished state, or perhaps because of it, our "monument" is quite the attraction for those visiting the Southland. "Spectator slowing" is commonplace, as all manner of tourists and sojourners will deliberately schedule a brief side excursion east along the freeway, away from the established entertainment attractions and amusement parks that garner fame in the Los Angeles area, to get a glimpse of the most famous unfinished project in Southern California!

Our church is right off Valentino Avenue at the top of the hill (after one passes the usual battery of commercial buildings—our bank, City Hall, Police and Fire Departments), where the avenue curves to the left in a directional change to the northwest. The church is on the corner of Ridgeway and Valentino Avenues. Our forefathers possessed enough foresight to obtain some sizable property for the church and its grounds, which can be clearly seen even at the bottom of the hill. As I have stated, the property is located directly 50 feet below the protruding chin of the legendary movie star. At the back of the property, a retaining wall butts up against the hillside as the mountains roll upward and eventually frame the famous face. This wall serves as the rear perimeter of the play area for our church's "King's Kids" Preschool, which includes all sorts of plastic forts and jungle gyms, as well as designated sand and grass areas. On some afternoons, the children literally frolic in the shadow of the chin and nose of the monument as it stretches over the play area, ominously staining the ground with shades of Hollywood lore as the sun sets.

In front of this designated recreational rectangle is our Educational Christianity building. This includes the class-rooms for the aforementioned Preschool, Primary Department (Kindergarten and 1st Grade), Grades 2 through 6, Junior High and High School meeting areas, as well as a full gymnasium. The Educational Christianity building was built 20 years after the main sanctuary, in the 1950s, as a result of a very large stock donation from an extremely affluent deceased member of the congregation. Even though the architecture is slightly dated (camouflaged with a brick veneer in an attempt to blend with the Worship Center), the large building remains quite functional and was well thought out in order to accommodate the large-scale adolescent population that beat up the walls, floors, and even ceilings on a daily basis.

The main sanctuary is a bit more awe-inspiring—even a bit pretentious. Not to be outdone by the Gothic-minded Lutherans, Presbyterians, and Catholics, who created such beautifully contrived, ornate modern-day cathedrals punctuating the communities in and around our Southern California area. As our suburban area sprawled and evolved, our church is the only religious facility within the actual town of Monument. All other faith opportunities are close enough but still officially outside the actual borders of the town. Our non-denominational forefathers spared no expense (and apparently had the cash flow to fund their dreams) in constructing a beautiful brick sanctu-ary, complete with a very high steeple.

Green grass and lovingly maintained flowerbeds wrap around the corner of the property at Ridgeway and Valentino Avenues. Cut right into the corner by two brick retaining walls are the steps that narrow as you climb to the awaiting path winding up to the main entrance. Large wooden double doors await to usher you into the lobby, which includes such a large vaulted ceiling and four evenly spaced, intricate wrought-iron hanging chandeliers that even King Arthur would have felt comfortable loitering around this regal entry hall. He might have felt a little more out of place, however, clanging his way into the actual Worship Center with his 6th-century buddies, as it embodies more of the traditional accoutrements of a conservative Baptist church.

Even though there are stained-glass windows (with abstract, vivid colors depicting vague, sacrosanct images serving as intermittent, tall sentinels between the paneled walls), the Worship Center tries to shed the lobby's Gothic first impressions and become a sanctuary devoid of as many distractions as possible, so that the members of Our Father's Evangelical Church can maintain their upward mobility and enter without hindrance into the very courts of our Namesake. Above and behind the Worship Center are all of the necessary practice rooms for the choir and musicians, as well as rooms for Adult Educational Christianity.

My very first recollection of the church includes no warnings or traveling images; I can merely recall in my mind's eye that I had been plopped down (like Philip and the Ethiopian) into the main meeting room of the 2nd- through 4th-grade Departments as an intimidated seven-year-old in 1965.

There are two sides to this colorfully decorated room, and the floor of each is filled with rows of those now famously traditional gray metal folding chairs. In my ignorance due to nervous tension, I did not notice that the room was segregated, with the boys on the right side and the girls on the left. Fortunately, perhaps by instinct, I gravitated to the correct side and quietly sat down next to another boy who was apparently also by himself. He was densely freckled, and tall and lanky for his age, with brown hair chocked full of cowlicks. His name was Glen Tollockson. He would become my new best friend at the church for the next two years. Regretfully, he moved away when we went into the 4th Grade, as his father had a job transfer out of state. I did my best at conjuring up a welcoming smile in spite of my extreme discomfort at the newness of it all. He turned to me and seemed to be responding in kind when—

"We are pleased to welcome Ian Block! I have known Ian's family for years. I even went to school with his grandfather!"

—my concentration was interrupted by the sandy voice of silver-haired Doris Mackintosh, Superintendent of the 2nd-, 3rd- and 4th-grade Departments. She looked like an older Ingrid Bergman, and I had the distinct impression she had been at this job since the church was built in the 1930s. She was married to Walter Mackintosh, a friendly, but slightly disheveled gentleman who has been an usher in the main sanctuary for as many years as Doris has presided over the 2nd-graders. She did, in fact, know my grandfather; they even dated occasionally in high school prior to my Grandmother Melba coming on the scene and permanently breaking up their intermittent romance! They have all remained friends even after my grandfather left our church.

After the usual singing (with the lyrics all colorfully printed out on poster boards that Mrs. Mackintosh held up in appropriate succession) and some announcements that I did not pay much attention to, Mrs. Mackintosh grabbed a wooden tripod leaning against the wall and placed it center stage. She then unfolded the two vertical halves of that eternally effective attention-grabber and retention solidifier—the flannel board! What the autoharp was to music in grammar schools, such has been the flannel board to education in Sunday schools.

When she was finished with her Bible story, another maternal, smiling, gray-haired assistant brought up a shoebox that was colorfully gift-wrapped. She held the box for Mrs. Mackintosh, who jammed her boney hand between the box and lid and pulled out a small, roughly cut square of colored construction paper that secretly divulged the row and seat number for the weekly "special seat" prize! The prizes were housed in yet *another* large gift-wrapped box in the corner of the meeting room, where the "chosen one" would lean over and carefully claw through the contents and extricate the toy of his or her choice. Over the weeks, it slowly dawned on me that the one "special seat" prize winner alternated week to week from the boys' side to the girls'. Having thus cracked this complicated code, I calculated the winning side for the next week—the girls'—and the following Sunday morning Glen and I rebelliously plopped down on the *left* side of the meeting room, mentally salivating at our ingeniously materialistic machinations that we had manufactured for raising our odds in intercepting the weekly prize from a potential *girl*.

However, Mrs. Mackintosh was not so easily duped, and before she had even started our church time, we were promptly escorted back to the right side of the room, proverbial tails between our legs, and were forced to humbly admit that our seemingly covert scheme wasn't so surreptitious after all!

When we graduated into the 3rd grade, we would leave the 2nd-graders (after the requisite songs and announcements) and march into one of six private Sunday school rooms off the common, main meeting room for our co-ed Bible lesson. I was then introduced to Mrs. Hawkins, who, over the next few weeks, introduced me to Jesus. Mrs. Mackintosh had planted and watered for a year, and Mrs. Hawkins knew a ripe harvest when she saw one. It seemed that I was the only one in the white field one Sunday, and the gardening tools had my name written all over them!

Mrs. Hawkins was an amenable, engaging senior citizen who strictly adhered to the proposed 3rd-grade biblical curriculum yet, over the next two years, had an uncanny ability to breathe historical life into the ancient tales. On this one watershed Sunday morning, she was relaying the story about the repeated callings to young Samuel during the night; she cleverly compared this heavenly hearkening with a beguiling picture of Jesus personally inviting children (much to the irritation of both close disciple and distant onlooker) to sit at his feet. She made the compelling case that the "caller" in both stories was one and the same.

I was hooked.

After the other children were excused from the room, Mrs. Hawkins wisely detained me as a result of discerning the longing look I had given her throughout the balance of her lesson, and proceeded to lovingly explain the Way, the Truth, and the Life to me. She concluded by reciting a heartfelt "sinner's prayer," which I sincerely echoed, line by line.

It seemed so simple then, the two of us in that 10 x 12 colorfully decorated Sunday school room. But little did I realize that the simply stated petitioning prayer of an eight-year-old boy, as it is with any new convert, reverberated through the expanse of heaven, rousing all manner of celestial beings—Cherubim, Seraphim, Archangels—into a celebration frenzy at the rescue of another soul. This joyful noise of triumph simultaneously ricocheted an "in your face" aftershock that shot out of the courts of God and slammed into the abysmal gates of Hell far below. All of this cataclysmic, cosmic profundity ripped through both hemispheres of the spirit world before I had even whispered, "Amen."

I confessed with my mouth what had occurred to Glen later, after the morning service. He responded that he had already prayed the "sinner's prayer" in the privacy of his bedroom at home some months before. It appears that his conversion never "took," or was never a cardiac commitment in the first place. I have kept in contact with Glen over the years, less now than when he first departed Monument. The last I heard, he was single, working for some delivery service in Tucson, Arizona. His body was laden with tattoos, and his unkempt apartment was shared by a rotating number of live-in women, who entered and exited through the revolving door of his bedroom with alarming frequency.

Glen was the first of many individuals and couples—scattered seeds—introduced into the chronology of my life, who, in their own subjective ways, have tasted that the Lord is good and yet would suddenly break away from the purview of their relationship with Him (and me!), no matter how deep and significant, and spin off into some skewed direction riddled with seemingly unnecessary trials and consequences, while the Father tossed all sorts of ignored attention-getters into their paths. While conversely, by the dogged, gracious grip of God, I continued chugging along the same track of my childhood faith, with a modicum of disruptive bumps, jolts, and metal screeching, in a linear direction toward my as yet unknown destiny. To paraphrase monarch and meteorologist Solomon (or, using his teacher *nom de plume*, "Qohelet"), as he sought to proclaim a sage ecclesiastical conclusion to his conundrum regarding the selectivity of certain righteous and unrighteous recipients for various seasons of rainfall, "Go figure!"

Commencement into a new grade has always been premature in the church. They seem to jump the gun by promoting you to a new level in June, prior to any preparatory summer vacation, where the mind and body can grow and adjust to the idea that, in three short months, come Fall, like the chrysalis of a moth, you will walk back into the public school and suddenly be a 5th-grader!

On that abrupt "Promotion Sunday" morning in June, I was walking up the grassy knoll of Our Father's Evangelical Church with my stocky brother, Owen. My parents had recently splintered off toward the main sanctuary and their respective Adult Sunday school class, we toward the Educational Christianity building.

As we hurried along, my concentration on just keeping up with my athletic brother was broken by his suddenly stating, "So, you're in 5th grade now, eh?"

"Yeah," I responded, slightly out of breath, as we made our way up the grade to the main entrance. "You're gonna have 'Synopsis Sid'!" he said.

"Huh?" I replied.

"*Synopsis Sid!*" he answered, slightly frustrated.

Not only was this *another* word I had to look up (I'm not even sure Owen knew what it meant), I had completely forgotten that I was now going to be a pupil of this widely known and highly appreciated 5th grade teacher. I remember my brother mentioning him on sparse occasions in the past, but, as he was four years older than me, it had been some time since the name had been mentioned.

"Who?" I asked.

But my brother had already waved me off dismissively and turned to go into the High School Department, where he had concerns of his own as a new freshman.

Although only down the hall, the 5th and 6th Grade Department was a world completely removed from the orbit of the 2nd-, 3rd- and 4th-graders. The new music was trendier. "The B-I-B-L-E," "This Little Light of Mine" and "I'm in the Lord's Army" had been replaced with the pulsating "King Jesus Is All," the snappy "I Am a C-H-R-I-S-T-I-A-N," as well as the routinely slower, contemplative songs like "It Only Takes a Spark," "Kumbaya," and "Oh, Magnify the Lord" (I have always found this phrase interesting. As if the Lord required any magnification in the first place! He's as big as He's ever going to get! I guess the magnifying glass must be held up solely for our benefit, positioned in such a way so as to aid us in enlarging Him to His "normal" size from our previously puny perspectives).

Mrs. Mackintosh's cassette player, which had been used to accompany our previous singing, had been replaced by a really "cool" kid named Rick (complete with tattered Levi jeans, and beaded leather necklace, from which dangled the catch-of-the-day, *ichthus*—that famous, Grecian aquatic symbol of the New Testament Underground), from the High School Department, who could play the three chords required on his guitar for our "worship time." After the opening ceremonies, the boys and girls were separately dismissed to their respective 5th- and 6th-grade Sunday school classrooms.

I was immediately introduced physically to the three other boys who would make up the balance of our class when we pushed open the door to our assigned small rectangle, Room B, and collided with and jostled one another for the best metal-folding-chair seats. Not that this was to any great advantage, as every seat in the house afforded an excellent view. We sat there, teacher-less, for what seemed like quite a long time—long enough for the silence to become palpable and uncomfortable. The blond boy in the

corner by the window broke the soundless barrier with the suc-
cinct, "My name's Nathan Raab. What's yours?" At that, we all
exchanged names (as only two members of the group knew each
other previously): "Kenneth Ball," "Patrick Hamilton," "Ian Block."

We were well on our way to some significant verbal ice-breaking
when the door suddenly opened and in walked "Synopsis Sid." It
was then that I realized why it took him so long to catch up with
his pupils, as he was an extremely rotund man. His ponderous
girth filled the doorway of Room B, eclipsing the fluorescent lighting of the main meeting room outside, as he grabbed both door
jambs and proclaimed, "Howdy, gents!" He used both grips to
push himself beyond the doorway and gain enough momentum to
collapse into the one seat facing us. He breathed out a sigh of both
relief and exhaustion as he filled and spilled over the now-rendered-
diminutive metal chair tenuously supporting his massive frame.

He was predominantly bald on top, with short, graying
brown hair wrapping around the sides of his globe-like head.
His jowls sagged down in such a way that, as they provided the
facial parenthetical to his plump, dipping chin, it looked like
three billowing curtains at the bottom of his jolly face, providing
a theatrical barrier for his unseen "performing" bow tie.

"My name . . . (he took another corrective gulp of oxygen) . . .
is Sid Barrington."

He paused.

With a suspenseful look of sly knowingness, he scanned over
the four of us with his congenial, small, dark eyes. He looked
down, causing his multiple chins to bunch into a stack of spare
tires under his jaw. He opened his large, dog-eared Bible about
three-quarters of the way through, where, sticking up like the
rudder of an overturned ship was a piece of white paper. He
picked it up with both hands and drew it close to his face. He

slyly peered up at us one last time over the top edge of the paper; then, after a brief clearing of his throat, he recited,

"A land mammal becomes a water rat while trying to outfox the Top Dog into using another guinea pig. Something smells fishy in the kangaroo court because the slothful scaredy-cat tries to weasel his way out of the doghouse. The king of beasts ferrets out the lion's share of the truth as the stubborn mule worms his way into confessing his bird-brained scheme that he doesn't want to be the gopher that gives snakes-in-the-grass bear hugs."

He looked up from the scrap of paper at four rapt faces of quadruple incredulity. Satisfied that he had our undivided attention, no matter how overwhelmed and confused, "Synopsis" Sid sought to expound on what had just been read with the invitation,

"Open your Bibles, boys, to the book of Jonah!"

Sid was married to Esmeralda Barrington. Her maiden name was Bertuccio, a full-blooded Italian with a family directly from Milan. They were physically the most mismatched couple at the church. She was petite, with sharp, dark eyes and wavy jet-black hair, impeccably dressed each week. They were an odd sight of opposites, a Q-tip and an egg. It begged the question that the longevity and quality of their 39-year marriage must certainly be fueled by the heart—which I guessed was as it should be. On first acquaintance with anyone at the church, Sid would predictably point up to the face of Rudolph and say with pride "I met Max Stellar one time when I was young. But if you want to know the real scoop on all the hubbub during the carvin', you should ask Doris [Mackintosh]; she is 15 years older than me and was around for the whole tadoo!"

The next week, Sid Barrington came lumbering into Room B dressed in a white shirt, with a rented black cape, top hat, and cane. He tossed his Bible onto his empty metal folding chair and remained standing, or, leaning against the chalkboard, as it were. This posturing was all for the sake of emphasis for the upcoming synopsis of the week. Sid Barrington standing in a 10 x 12 room was, indeed, emphasizing! He took off his top hat with a Houdini-like flair, turned it over, and reached in to pull out a piece of paper. Placing the hat back on his head and tapping the top for stability, he adjusted his behemoth body with as much prestidigitation as it would allow against the now-invisible chalkboard, leaned his left hand on the metal chalk holder, and recited the prose on the paper in his right hand with the gesticulating power and projection of a carnival barker (which undoubtedly penetrated through the walls into Sunday school classrooms A and C).

"The 'Moses Not-So-Magic Magic Act' is the best show in town! It has bested all the other acts on Rameses Street in the theater district of downtown Egypt. It sells out virtually every night because every night there are new wonders to behold! One night, there's hail coming down from the catwalks; another night, frogs come out of the orchestra pit; another night, a volunteer from the audience gets boils; another night, the drinking fountains in the lobby spurt out blood; another night, the lights mysteriously go out; another night, the theater is infested with flies and gnats, and the

concession stands make a killing on 'Off!' spray! On the closing night of the act, Pharaoh and his family are seen sitting in the official Dignitary Box. The night is a disaster, as Pharaoh cannot find his son after he leaves to go to the refreshment stand. Moses is forced to leave out the backstage exit. Pharaoh chases him to a nearby seaside resort where Moses, in a flash, performs his 'saw an ocean in half' trick and gets out of town. Pharaoh, in hot pursuit, quickly finds out that the act is all wet as the 'magic' wears off, and the joke's on him!"

Sid then took off his cape with a villainous twirl and coiled it onto an empty chair, placing his hat on the summit of the bundle. He then leaned his cane against the wall, picked up his Bible, and crashed down onto his chair. This revealed the chalkboard in its entirety for the first time since Sid had so audaciously entered the room. On the once-empty chalkboard was now mysteriously scrawled for the four eye-feasting Belshazzars of Room B,

"Turn to Exodus, Chapter Seven."

If Mrs. Hawkins breathed new life into the diverse popula-tion of the Bible, the characters of Sid Barrington were now cranium-marching around the inside curvature of my head! They were walking, talking, and performing their heroic or dastardly deeds over and over again, as they remained tethered to their individual legends originally gleaned from stone tablets, papyrus, and parchments.

So, off we went on another delicious romp through the Old Testament—Nathan Raab, Patrick Hamilton, Kenneth Ball, and myself. I felt like D'Artagnan and the Three Musketeers. We four were fast becoming very good friends Sunday after Sunday—"One for all, and all for One!" "United we stand, divided we fall!" However, our 17th-century fraternity pledges sounded and looked a whole lot more convincing when each of us used a deeper voice while one-arm saluting Bibles gripped and raised to the sky with our feet firmly planted atop metal folding chairs!

As usual, I sat with my mother and both grandmothers during the morning service after Sunday school (my father, ever the deacon, was to serve communion and would be joining us later). I, like young Timothy, was surrounded by my very own Eunice, Lois (and Lois!), whose purses were packed with gum-squared Chiclets and cherry Life Savers just to keep me occupied. Grandma Melba (small and frail), my dad's mom, and Grandma Frances (large and fleshy), my mother's mother, resembled two of the fairies, Flora and Fauna, from Walt Disney's 1959 cartoon, *Sleeping Beauty*. It would not grab me until much later in life the

absolute historical blessing of having two God-fearing generations as my rotating bookends each Sunday morning since my
earliest childhood memory. At my age, 11, I was more concerned
with a gradual fight for independence as I sought permission
to fly the pew-nest and sit with my friends. This cause was lost,
however, as the other Musketeers were also confiscated by their
own immediate families. It was a longstanding tradition at Our
Father's Evangelical Church that families sit together, if at all
possible. So, I resigned myself to creating my own "synopses"
on the back of the church bulletins—my own witty paragraphs
about Nehemiah, Ruth, and Judas (accompanied by my very own
cartoon depictions). Although they were pathetic attempts and
paled in comparison to the literally majestic master, I would,
however, be able to refine this craft over the years and perpetuate
this ministerial art form later in life.

One particular Sunday after our arrival at Our Father's
Evangelical Church, I found the seating arrangement in our
habitually designated pew to be oddly different. In between my
two grandmothers, my deacon father was already seated, next
to my mother, who was seated next to . . . Owen! At the closing hymn, when we four were all lined up according to height,
my father and mother suddenly peeled off during the second
stanza, followed by my brother, and all three headed down the
center aisle to officially join the church. One quick glance to my
right, and I saw the desertion taking place before my very eyes.
Having no foreknowledge of this decision, I scrambled past the
vacated seats and trotted down the center aisle in hot pursuit of
my family. My panic and exertion was all for nothing, however,
as I was apparently too young to join the church. I would have to
suffer my own private processional down the center aisle toward
church membership at a later date in my maturity.

In October, a good five months into our Sid Barrington tutelage, one very dark Sunday was filled with wicked surprise. I first detected that something was amiss by the 16mm Bell and Howell movie projector that was poised at the back of the 5th- and 6th-grade meeting room, aimed at a large white screen erected in the front. After the usual announcements, cool Rick led us in a bevy of what seemed to me to be a suspicious preponderance of droll music with commensurately dour lyrics. All in predestined preparation for the multimedia presentation that was to follow.

The movie was introduced as *For I Am Not Ashamed*, and, for the next 45 minutes, it took us on a visceral journey though the history of the persecution of the church. The film was not necessarily visually graphic, but, rather, by implication, coupled with the personal testimonies, the impact was harsh and ter-rifying. With aggressive Communism alive and well in 1969, in both west and east directions from our sea to shining seas, the most current verbal depictions of all manner of bullying, incarceration, and even the decapitation of loyal, belligerent Christians, the arresting stories from "surviving" missionaries not only served as a warning shot across the bow of the 5th- and 6th-grade Department, but also hit us broadside in the hull of our faith, ripping out a gaping hole of fear and horror.

After the movie, we were dismissed to our separate classrooms to discuss the film, only to find that Room B had a substitute teacher! The one person who might have provided a life raft for the four gasping Musketeers was unfortunately absent that week (Sid Barrington worked in real estate, and there was, apparently, a current housing boom in Southern California)! Our substitute was none other than Virgil Cronklin. Mr. Cronklin was a small, stooped man. He was a retired widower who seemed to harbor much bitterness over his current plight of combined inertness and aloneness. He wore an oversized light-brown suit (perhaps it was the correct size at the time of purchase, but Mr. Cronklin had shrunk over the years). His face looked like the top of a gourd, with all of the wrinkles stemming from his nose, as if they were magnetized from the outer reaches of his head. They spanned inward like the spokes on a bicycle wheel toward the hub. Under his full head of white hair, greased down and parted on the right side, Mr. Cronklin was a living, real-life definition of a crotchety old man!

What was meant to be an "afterglow" in an effort to augment the glowing embers of fright as 5th- and 6th-graders were given an opportunity to "talk it through," Mr. Cronklin slashed the intended agenda and took the opportunity to preach at us. Not only to reiterate the premise of the movie, but to personalize it by way of an obligatory application!!

"It's [persecution] going to happen—you can count on it!" he hissed in his ominous, raspy voice. The Four Musketeers were wide-eyed.

"The way things are going, it may happen in *your* lifetime!" Eight eyes wider.

"Maybe, even to you and your family!" Four mouths drop open.

Now, thanks to the spiritual horticulture of Mrs. Hawkins, I had suddenly found myself plunged into a life-threatening membership! Deep down inside, I knew that there was no alternative—all other ground being sinking sand and all—it was just that discovering the fine print of the eternal contract *after* the fact was acutely unnerving!

The next hour, I was very quiet while sitting next to my Eunice, Lois, Lois (and Seth), but as it was the expected behavior during the worship service, nothing was perceived as peculiar.

I could not create any synopsis that particular morning on the back of the bulletin. My mind was deadened, embracing only images of jungles, screams, and hammers and sickles. My emotions were welling up, and I was successful in suppressing them for only a short time. On the ride home from church, Owen thankfully dominated the conversation with a recap of the events from the High School Department, and I could remain pensive without attracting suspicion.

After our Sunday lunch, I escaped into the privacy of my bedroom. My mother came in after my absence from the common rooms of the house had aroused her curiosity; she found me lying on my back on my bed, thoughtfully looking up at the ceiling, with tears trickling down both sides of my face. "What's wrong, Honey?" my mother implored as she quickly closed the door behind her and sat down next to me on the side of the bed. I proceeded to tell her of the horrific events of that morning, losing my composure to greater degrees as the story progressed. My mother cupped her hand over my forehead, pushed back my hair, and wiped my cold, sweaty brow. She sought to soothe my shattered nerves by delivering a gentle, yet highly reassuring speech, not on the faith of martyrs, but on the military strength and political prowess of the land of the free and the home of the brave!

"That could never happen here," she confidently stated. "That may happen elsewhere, but not here! You can count on that, Ian!"

Once she had calmed my fears, she quietly slipped out of my bedroom. We never revisited the subject again, but I can imagine she was on the phone before I could blow my nose, chastising the powers that be at Our Father's Evangelical Church for their reckless irresponsibility in deciding appropriate subject matter for the 5th- and 6th-grade Departments, as well as their woefully lacking pool of substitute teachers! Her thrilling *E Pluribus Unum* speech to me, however, has stayed with me into adulthood. True, as a result of that fateful Sunday, I have always limped along when it comes to losing my life to save it. I am far more tempted, by fear, to save my life initially and risk the losing later. However, I have diligently tried to build muscles on my trust in a Heavenly Father who sovereignly presides over all manner of persecutions, light or intense. I have had to resign myself to the dubious fact that there is a method to His madness in doling out those individual cubit-sized life spans for each of us. That wisdom has been equally applied to martyrs like Peter and Paul, as well as the "taken up" likes of Elijah and Enoch.

But her patriotic consolation has had a great bearing on my political involvement as an adult, as I continue to play up my odds in my own small way by trying to make sure we continue living in a free country that can stem anti-Christian tides from within and without.

The next Sunday was a marked improvement and no less impactful. Synopsis Sid was back (after apparently selling all of the houses that he needed to), but he skipped his famous synopsis, as he had not had time to devise one the previous week. He dove right into the story of turncoat Balaam and his ass!! We could not keep straight faces at this *King James Version* wash-your-mouth-out-with-soap description of the famous talking beast of burden. Once the word had escaped the mouth of Mr. Barrington, prohibited jocularity simmered, boiled, surged upward, and was "dammed" up by our falsely stoic faces. We slowly made eye contact with one another, and, in an instant, our feeble defenses broke apart, and the guffaws came blasting out of our painfully pursed lips, filling Room B with quadraphonic belly laughs over the word "ass." Mr. Barrington seized the opportunity to make excuses for the word, historically whitewashing its inclusion into the King of England's *authorized* rendition as acceptable language in its day. All we heard was, "There's an *ass* in the Bible!" Mr. Barrington might have been relieved at the turn the derailed conversation was taking, as his lesson preparations seemed rather hit-and-miss that week. But the relief must have been replaced with equal discomfort as the conversation cascaded into a group session on the evils of all profanity in general. The best (or worst) part of the Sunday-school hour was that Mr. Barrington actually gave the class *permission* to say any four-letter word in question, as long as it was couched in a proper context (if there was such a thing!).

We couldn't believe our ears!

Fortunately, innate guilt confined our conversation to under-your-breath levels, lest we create an international incident in eavesdropping Rooms A and C. Earplugs must have been rapidly passed out in heaven while we bantered the origins of the "F" word and "S" word, as well as the apocalyptic, condemnatory "damnation" (with and without God's initiation).

We even discussed the odd notion that folks who blurted out "Jesus!" or "Christ!" or, if really angry, both first and last names, "Jesus Christ!" were swearing, to be sure. But why was God's Son the only lucky one to be included in the lexicon of profanity, whereas Buddha, Mohammed, Confucius, and the like, were conspicuously ignored? Was this an unconscious nod at the only Name with enough power and prestige to really matter? Was this a backhanded admission that *He* alone is worthy?

The four-letter (or five-, or six-) expletive freedom that was granted to us, for this hour only, never ceased to be uncomfortable for me. I was a party to something deceptive and unclean. But Mr. Barrington wisely concluded this spontaneous diversion (he, too, must have been squirming throughout—if you could only see it through his layers of natural padding) by suggesting that it might have been good to get this "out of our systems." However, there should be a finality to this deviant verbal behavior. He made a sound, adumbrated case that all of the profane words are:

Holiness Hitters: gluing "set apart" ones to the world's invective vocabulary with cookie-cutter precision.

Spirit Quenchers: causing the Spirit to be bathed in that which He is highly allergic to.

Father Disappointers: "Coarse joking," in all of its forms, does not look good on our adoption papers as "sons of God." And lastly,

Lazy: A more expansive, ready vocabulary does wonders for appropriate, instantaneous word substitution when the proverbial hammer hits the thumb.

We were satisfied, and we were convinced.

This highly explosive spontaneous dialogue that originated from the understandable heehaw of Balaam's ass, caused the four of us, as best we could, to think twice before allowing the four-letter words of our culture to find their way onto our palates. However, the *five* of us wisely agreed that we should keep the previous hour's discussion solely between ourselves, or there would surely be "Hell" to pay!!

My first kiss was planted on me when I was 15 years old. We were at the fourth and final stopover of our Junior High Christmas Progressive Dinner. We had swarmed like eighth plague locusts on the ill-prepared first three houses, devouring hors d'oeuvres, soup, salad, and a main course of spaghetti and lasagna.

The dessert stop was hosted at the home of our Junior High leaders, Tom and Jean Worrell. After dessert, we played a series of questionably seasonal party games, the last of which I had never played before and had the rather silly name of "Choo-Choo." Not only was the name silly—the plot was insipid as well. But the end result was scintillating! A boy and a girl were chosen to represent an engine and a coal car. The girl would place her hands on the hips of the boy engine in front of her and the two would begin chugging down the hall and through the house, making all sorts of embarrassing train noises. They would loop back to the roundhouse—the Worrells' expansive living room—and the engine would turn around and kiss the coal car, right on the lips! The coal car would then turn and scan the room, looking for a prospective caboose of the opposite sex. Once the new addition was conscripted, the newly lengthened train would again make its run around the house, only to stop again at the roundhouse and pass on the role of caboose. As the sequentially formed boy-girl-boy-girl "train" grew longer and longer, I found myself riddled with bullets of anticipation-perspiration.

My name was finally called by Tammy Wyngate, a short, slightly plump, blond-haired 8th-grader. Around the house, with my hands on Tammy's hips, I was nervously muttering "I think I can, I think I can." No one suspected any trepidation on my part as the chant artfully blended with the game's theme. Once we reached the roundhouse, the engine turned and kissed the coal car, and on down the train the lip-kissing cars continued. As the train was quite long by this time, the suspense was almost unbearable. Finally, Tammy turned to kiss me. Due to my newfound height, I had to awkwardly lean down to reach her face, which added fuel to my ignorance-induced embarrassment. When our lips finally met, the new sensation rushed through me so convulsively that Tammy quickly noticed that her caboose was stunned. Rather than risk being un-coupled for the next round because I swooned, I forcibly pocketed my shock and regained my composure; my lips scanned the room for another girl to be the new caboose.

I felt so blissfully affected in that moment when the lips of Tammy Wyngate pressed against mine. Christmas, 1973 will always have that sweet, first-time memory embracing it. At the very least, it certainly softened the chiding *"Sweet 16 and never been kissed"* barb that was later used, now unsuccessfully, to taunt me at my next birthday.

This electric feeling was duplicated on the day of my marriage to my beautiful bride, Maria. Due to our evening wedding in the winter of 1984, and the inarguable logistics of taking the obligatory photographs prior to the ceremony for "Let there be light" reasons, our wedding photographer, Marco, came up with a brilliant idea to preserve the significance of seeing each other for the first time in our wedding gear!

The first of the photos were to be shot in the waning sunshine on the lawn between the main sanctuary and the Educational Christianity building. The makeshift bride-bridesmaids', groom-groomsmen's dressing rooms had also been fabricated in the Educational Christianity building. Our photographer decided to orchestrate a private moment for the two of us in the hallway of the Educational Christianity building since we could not have the pleasure of seeing each other for the first time at the commencement of the actual ceremony.

He scheduled the bridesmaids-groomsmen photos first on the lawn, so that both separate dressing rooms were vacated, with the exception of Maria and myself. Once Maria was dressed in her wedding gown, Marco situated her in the hallway as I waited anxiously in my dressing room. He gently knocked on my door and quickly slipped out of the building to begin the photo shoot of the wedding party. I, the tuxedoed groom, opened the door. Standing there, framed in the downstairs hallway of the Education Christianity building of Our Father's Evangelical Church, was the most spectacularly gorgeous woman I had ever seen. She was truly radiant—the very adjective Christ gave for his future bride. I walked up to Maria and took both of her hands in mine. I do not remember what was said. Perhaps nothing. Our loving, devoted sentiments were clearly expressed in our mutual gazes upon one another.

Maria then suggested that we go into one of the side rooms and pray over the monumental evening that was looming. We arbitrarily opened a door to my right, and I found myself in the meeting room of the 2nd-grade Department that I had first stepped into 19 years before, in 1965. We sat down on two small, blue plastic chairs designed for very small children, as the room had been converted to accommodate the Primary Department (Walter and Doris Mackintosh had long since moved away to a retirement community). At the proportionately small activity table, we held hands and prayed to the Third Strand in our forming cord to bless and protect our forthcoming union and the completely new life that it would instigate.

When we were finished, we engaged in more longing looks that spoke volumes. Our trances were dispelled by a soft knock on the door as Marco, considerately giving us as much private time as possible, now needed Maria for the first of myriad wedding-picture combinations.

We passionately kissed each other for the last time as singles, and Maria softly glided out of the room. When the hydraulic hinge had completed its task of gently shutting the door again, I was left alone in the meeting room until my mug shot became necessary outside.

I looked around the room, at the colorful Bible pictures, the numerous pinned-up awards, even a giant thermometer drawn on a large swath of white butcher paper (with thick, black, horizontal lines and numbers portioning off the picture—showcasing a contest of some sort) tacked up with the scattered individual name tags of the current Sunday occupants, a large, beige supply cabinet, a puppet theater folded against the wall. My mind could hear the faint sounds of a pinball machine: the deep rolling sound of the ball; the ringing of bells; the staccato clapping of the protective flippers. This distant cacophony gradually became infused with other, closer sounds, as these walls that could talk paraded before my mind an auditory retrospective of a seven-year-old boy who was about to get married!

My mind could hear the booming voice of Sid Barrington, standing in front of us in an unusually crisp, neatly pressed, portly tailored blue business suit, carrying a capacious black briefcase, out of which were bulging numerous, disheveled mock contracts and various other elongated corporate documents:

"After breaking the specifically spelled out contractual agreement regarding a forbidden tree, Adam and Eve find themselves lawfully terminated from Paradise with a severance package loaded with Fallen World legalese as a constant reminder for them to 'enhance their resumes' with future serpent resistance. So the Garden of Eden goes under new management after an unsuccessful, hostile reptilian takeover bid. A Security Guardian Angel is posted at the automatic doors of the Tigris-Euphrates Corporation. These remaining two stockholders are bought out and are permanently discouraged from looking back over their shoulders and entertaining thoughts of living in a past that has gone into Chapter 11 (actually, it's Chapter Three)."

I could hear the murmurs, rustling, and general commotion expanding in ever-widening circles on the left side of the Worship Center, as Deacon Holbert had stumbled over a snag in the carpet on the side aisle during communion. He was just about to serve wealthy Tatiana Kincaid, who was wearing a smart new pant suit that was yes, white! His torso took the brunt of the sacred tsunami as he protectively turned on instant reflex, but the ensuing splattering of grape-juice buckshot found its way around Deacon Holbert and peppered Ms. Kincaid with a lasting memory of the holy sacrament. Her outfit truly looked like it had the chicken pox when she furiously exited the building that morning.

I could hear the sound of my own surprised gasp of betrayal as I caught my first supposedly "steady" girlfriend kissing a fellow staff member behind a rack of robes in the choir room in 1972, when we all worked at the church's "Fun in the Son" Summer Day Camp. I was certainly *not* the one having "Fun in the Son" that day!

I could hear the delighted high-pitched shrieks of hundreds of children as they made their way through our church's annual "Haunted House" on Halloween Night. As a junior in high school, I was employed to play creepy "Phantom of the Opera" music on the organ that was transplanted into one of the many-partitioned vaults, dungeons, attics, and graveyards of the completely converted "haunted house" gymnasium. My part could be played devoid of actual talent as one only had to roll his fists over the keys of the two manuals on the organ while simultaneously stomping his feet on the bass pedals haphazardly in order to produce the discordant sound reminiscent of horror-movie scores. Complete with creaking doors, vampires, opening coffins, rooms crawling with plastic spiders and snakes, and a surprise slippery slide from a 2nd-story staircase as the only means of escaping, Our Father's Evangelical Haunted House packed in mobs of kids from all over the town and beyond. Even though the tradition has faded into a more conventional Fall Carnival, I wonder who would be turning over in their graves now if the original event were resurrected!

I could hear the sound of my own heavy breathing as I frantically tried to appease the respiratory needs of my quaking junior high body as I lay on the driveway, jammed against the wheel well, underneath the Senior Pastor's car after our multi-bodied, full-scale T.P. attempt of his home was aborted midway by his suddenly turning the porch light on. His fuzzy brown slippers were inches away from my head as he walked out and stood in his bathrobe, scrupulously surveying his front yard for culprits.

I could hear the peals of laughter among the self-appointed matchmakers around the long restaurant table as the budding romance of the church's most eligible bachelor and bachelorette ended up flat on its back. They were getting on in years and over previous relationships, so it behooved Sam Morley to make his first move at the restaurant we visited after the Sunday evening church service. He slyly reached up his right arm to the back of Betsy Lambert's wooden parlor chair. His hand clasped the curved wooden railing of the back of her chair at the same instant that Sam became desperately aware that he had greatly miscalculated the shift in weight, and both chairs went straight back onto the floor of the restaurant. Like two astronauts seated for takeoff, the shocked fledgling couple just lay there in sitting positions, feet in the air, looking straight up at the ceiling, as one of our group's many comedians quipped, "Nice move, Sam—way to sweep her off her feet!"

I could hear the sound of 6th-grade snickers as the Four Musketeers were crouched down outside in their underwear behind a hedge by the window of the Educational Christianity building after having just staged the rapture of Room B. Taking full advantage of Mr. Barrington's perpetual lack of punctuality, we stripped off our clothes and laid them carefully out in sitting positions on our respective metal folding chairs. Preoccupied Synopsis Sid had already sat down before he noticed, in the twinkling of an eye, that his pupils had mysteriously disappeared! His Pre-Tribulation mind strained in panic as he endeavored to move his Mid-Tribulation body off the chair to get to the door and check outside to see if the Post-Tribulation folks were wrong!

Yes, indeed, this is the church!

CHAPTER TWO

THIS IS THE STEEPLE . . .

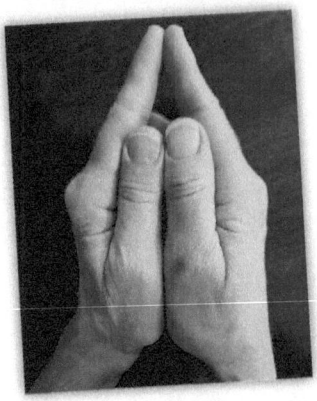

"Look up!" barked the obnoxious guide into the static-filled microphone to the passengers of our special, tourism-designed bus as it careened through the glass and steel canyons of downtown Manhattan.

"There's the Empire State Building! Look up!"

"There's the Chrysler Building! Look up!"

"There's the World Trade Center! Look Up!"

Our necks were craned into a horizontal position for the majority of the three-hour tour of New York as we "looked up!" through the strategically placed roof window running along the spine of the dirty, rectangular vehicle. Maria and I did not have level eye contact again for weeks.

Our "back East" tour had been my brilliant idea. We had yet to have any children, so I thought a traveling adventure for the two of us, celebrating over a year's worth of marriage, would be just the right ticket (although the Greyhound pelting exhaust all over the City That Never Sleeps was a low ebb in the brainy excursion). Although "Look up!" quickly became a running joke over time between Maria and me, as we would loudly beckon one another skyward for any laughable cause!

However, our rental-car meanderings north from New York to Boston revealed a far more subtle invitation to "Look up!" Most of the quaint, provincial towns that dot the Eastern Seaboard have, as their civic centerpiece, a colonial church with an unashamed steeple pointing the way.

This raising of architectural hands provided a profound image as steeples were visible all along the lush river valleys and green rolling hills of the original colonies. A Puritan rebuttal to the pagan obelisk. Like intermittent Mordecais standing tall amidst a sea of bowing cowards in a singular refusal to pay homage to Haman.

By merely looking at the scenery beyond our car window, and observing the obviously drawn conclusions, we, too, would absorb this admonition in life to "Look up!"

Even in the comic-strip world, all manner of citizens of Metropolis—rich, poor, old, young, religious, atheist, or agnostic—would walk toward a gathering crowd on the city sidewalk with their heads tilted back and, by automatic reflex, do likewise so as to ascertain the source of their fascination. Everyone would be "looking up" as Superman displayed his superhuman strength by lifting a mangled helicopter that had crashed into the side of a skyscraper hundreds of feet above the rapt, weak, human population below.

Is there such real-life amazement when and if the crowd sees the Almighty working in me?

A battery of tests to that end would soon be forthcoming.

A. W. Tozer was aware of the fence-walking dilemma pressing upon believers when he offered this classic observation to those attempting a serious Pursuit of God: "One of the greatest hindrances to internal peace which the Christian encounters is the common habit of dividing our lives in two areas, the sacred and the secular."

It can make you feel like an expendable cast member in the imperial Roman games as you feel the chains that are clamped at your wrists grow taut when each arm is stretched by two colossal, specially selected beasts, "In the World" and "Not of the World"—the strongest of the menagerie caged below—as they pull in opposite directions on the dirt floor of the sold-out, chanting arena.

I would feel this polarization every time I got out of bed and set foot in the faithless world that surrounded me.

Monument, California, by evolution and coincidence, *did* inadvertently recreate that colonial feeling as the steeple of Our Father's Evangelical Church lifted the cross of Christ much higher than Golgotha in a long-standing attempt to provide direction for planet Earth inmates much further than the two "darkening the door" experiences of

Christmas:

"The wool is pulled over the eyes of Herod when Wise Men deliberately ditch on the king's request for the whereabouts of the Lamb of God. As a result of not having a 'Map to the Star's homes,' Herod goes on a murderous rampage of child endangerment, not once stopping to ask for directions or call information about new relocations in Egypt."

and Easter:

"A body is missing. A massive tombstone has been removed by unseen hands. Visions of angels have been circulated by some fanatical aficionados of the victim. A government cover-up of 'unauthorized exhuming of the deceased' is devised. There are no clues, no smoking gun, no fingerprints, no ransom note. Neither is there a manhunt, red alert, APB, or milk-carton pictures. All seems safely swept under the carpet until more than 500 people confidently yell, 'Resurrection!'"

From the freeway, the steeple did, in fact, seem to symbolically proclaim this edict from the top of our gradual hill.

Conversely, the Rudolph Valentino backdrop above and beyond our Calvary hat-tipping, 40-foot-high directional signal, was not providing as much inspiration. The tip of Rudolph's nose had cracked off during the Southern California Sylmar earthquake of February 1971. Our house, about a mile from the church, shook so violently I thought God had grabbed our humble abode by the collar and was trying to knock some sense into it. My brother, Owen, slept through the whole thing! My father and mother, in complete ignorance of proper post-earthquake procedures, ushered us all quickly outside onto the front lawn in a quest for safety from the potentially collapsing house, thereby risking our traversing over broken glass and falling knickknacks, not to mention the potential of encountering serpentine electrical wires snapped off from stubborn telephone poles!

Fortunately, their inexperience at preparedness in the first large earthquake in recent memory did not end up causing life-and-limb damage to any of the Block family. When the phones had regained consciousness, ours began ringing immediately. Twice- and thrice-removed family members from all parts of the country were now our closest friends, caring about every gory detail, be it accurate or contrived, of our recent geological trauma.

One call was from Deacon Holbert, who lived right next door to the church. He had quickly walked over to check out the perilously predominantly brick campus. "There's no significant damage that I can see," reassured Deacon Holbert to my fellow deacon father after he had completed his cursory inspection of the church property. My father hung up the phone, relieved that he could now singularly focus on our own home and emotions and not have to divide his attentions with Our Father's Evangelical Church.

The phone rang again.

It was Deacon Holbert again. He reiterated that there was no damage to the church proper, however, the "King's Kids" Preschool play yard was filled with all sizes of granite chunks. In spite of the high retaining wall, the tip of Rudolph Valentino's nose had fallen from his face, hit the mountain below, and exploded into thousands of pieces. Some of these nose bits had rolled down the mountain and bounced over the wall of the church property, smacking into play equipment and bursting into still-smaller granite fragments, until the play yard looked like it was ready for a Flintstones' Easter Egg Hunt.

It took our custodial staff, along with a few other volunteers, quite a while to clean up the play yard. "King's Kids" Preschool was canceled for the rest of the week, lest more of Rudolph's face crack off during an aftershock and pummel the plastic jungle gym while replete with dangling simian pupils.

The half-Sheik carved in the mountain, with his truncated proboscis, now looked more like a half-Sphinx. This then made the elevated cross in front all the more imperative, as it sought to visually stem the tide of our accidental tribute to polytheistic ancient Egypt!

My tide-stemming started in a tide pool. Like tadpoles and other simple-celled organisms that mill about like amphibious automatons in the liquid incubator of a stagnant pond, so were the saved and the unsaved indistinguishable within the parameters of my elementary-school experience. The only distinction for me was the derogatory verbal volley playfully thrown at me of the grossly overused barb, "Blockhead!"

In the last half of the 1960s, childhood ran its normal course. Elated curiosity at the world around us, and even the introduction of the three "R"s fostered a willful receptivity to the intellectual regimentation that began at the John Adams Elementary School of Monument, California, for a brand-new crop of human beings fresh off the production line some five years before. It was a wonderful seven-year experience for me. From my mother taking me into my kindergarten room and my new teacher pinning a red, elephant-shaped name tag to my shirt bearing the big, black felt-tipped-pen letters, IAN, to getting all dressed up in the latest fashions of the new 1970s decade for our 6th-grade graduation ceremony in the charming, old-fashioned mahogany school auditorium.

I was able to walk to school when I reached the 3rd grade, as the two-story, colonial brick John Adams Elementary School was only seven blocks from our home on *Vista* Street (the last thoroughfare vestige of the town's prior name). I rode my purple three-speed, banana-seat Schwinn Stingray bicycle down the hill to school in 5th and 6th grade. No fences, no gates, no locks. For a brief time, the Christian and non-Christian worlds were an amalgam of tandem morality, responsibility, ethics, and duty. These muddied worldviews did not noticeably reveal combative growing pains until I reached the cusp of adolescence and the academic threshold presented to me at the Monument Junior High School.

Unintentionally, my set of friends from the John Adams Elementary school were completely rotated with a brand-new set as the plethora of divergent opportunities of the middle-school galaxy attracted each of us in his own way as motivated by our bents and interests, which were now manifesting themselves with increasing overtness.

Even my friends and I at Our Father's Evangelical Church were swept up in the undertow of an exchange program that we did not see coming. The Four Musketeers, with their stolid commitment to solidarity, found themselves calling it quits as the church's Junior High Department cajoled Nate, Pat, Ken, and me to four opposite points of the puberty compass.

My brother Owen had provided his trailblazing services four years in advance for the second Block boy as I made my journey through the Monument Public School system. He did, however, toss a couple of forks in the road that forced me to deviate. First and foremost because he was highly athletic, built for any and all sporting events, and thereby excelling in popularity and prowess under the proud heading of "jock." By comparison, I was a sorry disappointment as I gravitated to a more artistic path. I was tall for my age, but my penchant for reading, writing, and drawing took precedence over any budding basketball career. So Atlas preceded Aristotle as the

Block boys made their mark on the educational system of Monument, California.

It is interesting—the brotherly barriers that can be built up over the years. Even though Owen and I had our own separate rooms on Vista Street (a direct result of parental foresight at our extremely divergent personalities and interests), we still harbored a propensity for sibling rivalry and would jump at the chance to "best" each other whenever the opportunity presented itself. I can vividly remember a truly *watershed* incident when this one-upmanship reached an all-time low at my expense!

I was 11 years old at the time, in the middle of taking my evening shower, when my dad called Owen to his bedroom on the other side of the house. He was lying on his bed, reading the paper, and asked Owen to retrieve me, as he wanted to speak to me on some pressing matter. Owen, knowing I was "indisposed" at the moment, tried to explain this to my father. But my 1950s "speak only when you're spoken to" father would have none of my brother's explanations of my whereabouts or in what I was supposedly engaged. He became more insistent as my brother persisted, until finally Owen capitulated to my father's now-very-stern demands. So, empowered by the permissive behest of big daddy, Owen marched across the house with a determined, "OK, you asked for it!" fixation of his jaw. He barged into our bathroom and ripped back the shower curtain like a psychotic Anthony Perkins. I was no match for my 15-year-old brother's brawny strength, and he violently pulled me out of the shower and dragged me, struggling and slippery, across the house to my parents' bedroom. He proudly presented his younger brother to his father: "Here he is, Dad, just like you asked!"

My father looked up from the newspaper and saw his smug oldest son tightly clasping his younger brother's arms behind his back. His youngest son was standing there, buck-naked, dripping wet!

My dad completely forgot why he had originally wanted me in the first place and burst out laughing at the spectacle before him. My brother joined in, still firmly holding back my arms. My mother even came in from the kitchen, curious to see what all the jocularity was about. When she saw me standing there in an enlarging puddle on the carpet, she, too, could not help herself at uncontrollable, gleeful howling. The Streaker, however, was not even cracking a smile. I was not only dripping wet—I was dripping with pre-pubescent humiliation and shame.

It is strange how the pranks and antics of childhood and adolescence become so neatly stacked, like a deck of cards, over time. They can then be dealt out with precision to now-adult family members, determining the roles they still fall into like ruts: their behavior toward one another, their communication styles, and the mental games they play. Even the threat of competing, embarrassing-information ammunition from living together for so many years lurks directly under the floorboards and can be unearthed by any family member at the slightest provocation.

Such was the "Venus and Mars" relationship between Owen and me.

By wicked coincidence, or sheer twist of fate, I rarely saw any of my other friends or acquaintances from Our Father's Evangelical Church in the public schools. Either our paths never crossed due to scheduling differences, or they had been consigned to other schools in the district by virtue of where they lived. Our district on Vista Street offered three schools conveniently adjacent to one another—a "Triple Crown" of successive institutions in the business of molding minds of mush. John Adams Elementary, and Monument Junior and Senior High Schools were wisely bunched together as planned by a slow-growth-desirous City Council. They were also nicely blended with the same two-story, colonial brick architecture. By the time I was enrolled, various creeping vines had made their way up a significant portion of the outside walls, giving our tripartite school district an academic, Ivy League, East Coast aspect.

The first sign of tearing up the faith-faithless infrastructure came in my 7th-grade Science class, when Mrs. Carden began teaching Evolution *by assumption*. To be sure, she scattered the word "theory" throughout her lecture, but she might just as easily have licked a postage stamp-sized sign with the word "mouse" on it and stuck it on the forehead of the giant, invisible elephant sitting in the middle of the classroom! It was that obvious that "theory" was a condescending courtesy at best. I looked around the classroom for any other "You've got to be kidding!" faces and found none. All eyes were riveted on the teacher as she spun the most outrageous web of implausible lunacy with the audacity of calling it "science." The class obsequiously nodded their automaton heads in brain-dead agreement. These pollywogs actually believed they had hopped out of the pond by themselves! They even went so far as to ask what they perceived to be intelligent questions, also couching their inquiries with the proper quota of the word "theory," so as not to offend any religious zealot who might be planted in the room who still believed in the fables and fairy tales spoon-fed them by some hocus-pocus Creationist cult, namely me!

The tearing continued until the widening fault line was right underneath my feet! I did what I shamefully thought any red-blooded, Bible-thumping, lone 12-year-old boy would do to preserve his tenuous reputation and prevent any persecution or ridicule—I leaped over the gaping Evolution chasm to the pollywog side! Superman did not rescue any crashed helicopters that day! The writer to the Hebrews had a "scientific" word for this bowing to peer pressure bubbling over in the test tube of Chapter Ten—I had *shrunk*! Given what I knew to be true, I could have dropped down on all fours and, like Toto, pulled back the curtain on Mrs. Carden's *Wizard of Oz* textbook lecture to reveal the lever-pulling, button-pushing smoke screen that it actually was.

But I did not.

My pointed steeple was a flaccid embarrassment that day.

The pollywog side of the canyon was more comfortable. That should have come as no surprise to me. I was no longer a threat to any principalities and powers as I looked back over my shoulder to the other side of the abyss to see my discarded armor of God piled in a heap at the edge. My newfound junior-high friends in the public school did not suspect any religiosity emanating from chameleon Ian Block. They knew I went to church (I had somehow leaked that out under my breath). As I have stated, Our Father's Evangelical Church was the only one in town and highly visible up there on the hill, so my friends were definitely aware of its existence. But my weekend behavior was as irrelevant to my junior-high compadres as having a Salem witch five generations back in your family's past.

Group mentality held the day Monday through Friday. On Sunday mornings, I would go into my closet and don my *other* hat: Christian Boy. Without that heavy armor of God to impede my trajectory, I became quite agile at canyon crossing. My behavior was so finely tuned that I maintained bona fide family member-ships with both the Hatfields and McCoys while neither side was privy to the traitor in their midst! My Dennis the Menace parents were oblivious to the foibles of their two-faced son and, as a result, did not ask many probing questions. Traditionally, they only responded from their busy routines to interruptive, catastrophic family situations when either the roof was falling in or the bottom was dropping out.

The only one not fooled by the criss-crossing of these bloodlines was the omniscient, omnipresent, omnipotent Guy who had adopted me in the first place. From a place of rock-solid security and confidence in His beginning a good work in me and its ultimate completion on the day of Christ Jesus, He watched as yet another moronic, wayward sheep went astray, turning everyone to his own way, dispatching as many angels as were necessary to surround the Prodigal, depending upon the level of spiritual stupidity to which he had shrunk.

I even found myself taking leadership responsibilities within my two groups of friends and acquaintances from "church" and "world." At Our Father's Evangelical Church I was an "on fire," consistent attendee, and point man on Sunday mornings and midweek Bible studies. I was even finally baptized with much anticipatory pomp and circumstance.

At Monument Junior High School, I also rose to a capacity of Tribal Chief. I was creative (a cartoonist for the school yearbook), a fairly compelling talker (speech-making, in all of its forms, seemed to come naturally for me), and funny (I was voted Class Clown at the end of my 9th-grade year), as I sought to countermand the prestigious four-year-old paper trail left by the other star Block brother.

As God would see to it, my anchor in all this vacillating was a small plot of land about three blocks north of the church. The simple, two-bedroom, tan home of Melba and Colby Block. My father was an only child. My parents were married in 1951, after a whirlwind romance and accelerated courtship through the halls of Monument High School and the San Fernando Junior College, after my mother's family had moved to California from Tampa, Florida, in 1948. Nancy Benjamin was one of two daughters of Carl and Frances Benjamin. Sylvia, my mother's older sister, was equally yolked to a wealthy non-Christian whose business was still in Tampa. Consequently, we never saw Aunt Sylvia, Uncle Bob, or their family very often.

As Owen was so wrapped up in walking and leaping and praising coaches, he did not spend much time with his four grandparents. So it seemed, by process of elimination, that I was to be the only grandson to be focused upon by Grandma Frances, Grandpa Carl, Grandma Melba, and Grandpa Colby— four loving, God-fearing grandparents who vicariously wore my shirked armor of God for me.

Colby Block, the obvious patriarch of our brood, determined that I should gain a sound work ethic, as he had acquiesced to the role of spiritual advisor to his deacon son and his daughter-in-law. He was well-versed on the subject, as he had lived through two World Wars (he had fought in the first one over in France somewhere), the oddly re-named Korean *Conflict*, the Depression, and countless cycles of life experiences, only to extract one meaningful creed soaring out of the whole multi-faceted span of his 70-plus years on Planet Earth—from the Wright Brothers to Neil Armstrong—that "hard work never killed anybody!"

Now that the death threat had been eliminated, I had no excuse not to agree to my first paying job—doing yard work every Saturday for my grandfather. Even though his small piece of property was being encroached upon by a constantly growing and modernizing town, he gave the impression (with his John Wayne cowboy hat, ripped and patched faded plaid flannel shirt, black boots, and a perspective reaching back to 1895 to his birthplace only a few miles from where we were standing), that the 20 x 20 lawn I was about to mow with his antediluvian Toro lawnmower might as well be some endless field in Montana. The lawnmower was his plow. He exuded such convincing historical ebullience as he stood there, like Don Quixote, proudly gazing at his lawn and the soon-to-be-emasculated shrubbery of his home on the range, where the deer and the antelope play, where seldom is heard a discouraging word . . .

During his diligently decreed, torturously brief break times, sitting on one of the three steps of the front porch, hemmed in by an ornate wrought-iron railing, sipping cans of chilled 7-Up that my Grandmother Melba had sensitively absconded with from the kitchen refrigerator and offered to us, I would be able to chat with my Grandfather about anything and everything that came to mind.

Of course, Ian "Pandora" Block wanted to pull off that shroud of mystery that fogged up the rearview mirror of Our Father's Evangelical Church!

"Grandpa, why don't you come to church anymore?"

Nonplussed, he pushed back his cowboy hat, revealing the first tuft of his close-cropped white hair with stadium-sized widow's peaks, looked directly into my eyes (optical wanderings were either rude, lazy, or indicative of hiding something in my Grandfather's estimation of communication disorders), trolling deeply below the surface of my question, he finally broke off his gaze, focusing forward at the Mohawk-sporting lawn, and waved off the question when his mind had returned from racing into the past for a rhyme or a reason.

"Sycophants!" he muttered absently, as if still firmly transported back to that fateful night and reiterating his obdurate pronouncement. He then shook his sweaty head as if to erase the controversial drawing on the Etch-A-Sketch of his mind's eye, slapped both of his knees with his hands, and got up from the porch, announcing, "Come on, Ian, drink up! We've got a lawn to finish."

The Saturday anchor with Grandpa Block infused me with a breadth of stability I would otherwise have missed, and floundered. Even though his conversations were at times laconic, curt, and dismissive, others were "long drinks of water," as he called them. These recitations would include: his version of the history of Monument, or stories about his father (and his Civil War exploits at 16 years old!), his mother (who had eight children!), his brothers and sisters (of which he was the youngest), what it was like living with Grandma Melba for more than 50 years, how to succeed in business, and, overall, the mandate of honesty and integrity running from top to bottom and down every corridor of life—which cut like a two-edged sword as I was soul-stabbed right in the middle of my own double standards. Nevertheless, I was *his* charge, by hook or crook.

While round-faced, muscular, short, curly brown, Julius-Caesar-haired Owen Block was making touchdowns and setting high-jump records, I was drinking 7-Up every Saturday after turning my Grandfather's front lawn into a golf green, wrestling with tenacious vines of ivy, or jamming a suppository garden hose into plugged-up pipes and flushing out the bowels of plumbing underneath his house, and confidently understanding that I was completely connected and accepted, body, soul, and spirit, with a previous generation.

It was a pity that I did not give the same opportunity for camaraderie to all of my friends at Monument High School. In my micromanaged, godless sphere of influence on campus, I continued in my anti-Owen behavior (Class Clown again, as well as Most Artistic!), without the wisdom of checking my decisions with the Wonderful Counselor. I did not buckle to the usual known vices of profanity, drugs, or sex. However, in order to compensate for this innate foundation of conscience, poured by Our Father's Evangelical Church so many years before, and to hide it from my friends, I did my best at covering the slab with the weeds of rebellion. I had grown wicked in my cutting sense of humor and overly confident in the expendability of my friends.

On any particular day, unannounced, this God-shaped void could be flooded to a new level of cruelty as I arbitrarily deemed a member of our group an outcast. A good reason (if there ever was one) was not a prerequisite for the expulsion of another human being from the security of our cadre. Whether you looked the wrong way or had body odor, it was not important, as your name was casually drawn in my cruel lottery devised from the pit of Hell. You simply woke up one morning, went innocently to school, and found your locker vacated by your friends and all communication lines perniciously severed from those who had talked and laughed with you 24 hours earlier. All by the wielding and pointing of the irresponsible leader's scepter. I held in my hands the keys to our wicked little kingdom and locked people in or out with the flagrant whims of my darkened will.

The relational carcasses in my adolescent wake are an egregious scar on my life to this day. I now cherish devoted, loyal friendships and will for the rest of my life. I also try to sincerely *be* one.

Following in my parents' footsteps, coupled with my insecurities and indecision regarding what college to attend (to no one's shock, Owen had received an athletic scholarship from a school back East), I decided to enroll at the community college in the San Fernando Valley, along with my remaining friends from Monument High School after our graduation in 1976.

In order to pay for my weekend expenditures (gas for my 1974 Ford Mustang, fast food, concerts, and movies), it was necessary for me to secure another job beyond the yard work provided by Grandpa Colby.

I first worked at a Christian radio station, on the technical side. But the job grew monotonous in spite of the many spiritual perks that were part and parcel of a non-profit Christian organization and its dedicated employees.

I then landed a job in a department store that was the anchor for the first brand-new, large-scale indoor mall experiment in the Southern California area. It was a few miles outside the quaint town of Monument, but it might as well have been a million.

It was high time I began collecting on the dividends of faith investments made by my family and church over so many years and regain my strength in the name of the Lord. So, I sought to take on the fallen world of retail clothing with intrepid salt and light fervor.

The department-store denizens are a colorful lot. Everyone from nice, part-time old ladies just eking out a little extra cash to offset the paltry pittance bestowed upon their retired husbands by the government, to the corporate shark in the making—that flawlessly dressed "hear me roar" woman who bulldozes her way into upper management, making sure that every employee in her path is making their share of the almighty dollar (does He *really* want His name attached to currency?), every rack of clothing neatly displaying the latest fashion, and every mannequin dressed to the hilt and positioned to look like they are really enjoying themselves.

Shoplifters, shopaholics, temperamental design artists, fashion consultants, buyers, sellers, money lovers, corporate red tape, Christmas decorations in October, interminable exchange lines, stacks of clear-packaged T-shirts and underwear, wheels of neatly pressed suits, hooks sagging under the weight of multiple belts capable of wrapping around any global or invisible waist lines.

The new and improved "Daniel" Block had unknowingly walked into a Babylonian lions' den.

Among the cast of characters who swarmed the honeycomb of the three floors that made up the department store was an openly gay employee named Sergio. Sergio both looked and acted the part of androgynous purveyor of Men's Sportswear. Although rampantly lost, he had a very quick wit. My first encounter with one supposedly from *another* orientation was both sweet and sour. Dressed in a tight-fitting, jewelry-bedecked style that made any assumptions about his attractions completely unnecessary, Sergio could have me doubled over with laughter one minute, and the next clucking my tongue from afar at the "speck"tacle of it all as I cast my plank-ridden eyes on him and wondered in perplexity and vexation at the massive misdirection and misconceptions at play here. All those presumed "straight" friends of mine, both Christian and not, who eventually came out of their respective closets and were forced to seek refuge with their own kind because the church could not help itself in falling in step with the *only* expedient remedy it knew (as it had been applied in the past to biblical leprosy): head-in-the-sand ostracism. As a result, a subterranean battle is being waged in this area on many different fronts, as new generations cope with living, working, eating, drinking, laughing, and crying having had experienced a parental deficiency of some sort, whether numerically or emotionally, with not enough demonstrative affection from either sex to properly punctuate their childhoods.

No wonder the probably single Apostle Paul included this particular lifestyle in his Corinthian litany of inherent, pervasive behaviors to be *expected* from a fallen nature yet not *permitted* in the kingdom of God. Then he pulled the rug out from underneath any "holier than thou" ones with the sweeping leveler, *"and such were some of you!*—the "you" providing the right dose of chastisement and humility, the past tense "were" providing the hope of a way of escape.

Regardless, even one of the supposed "righteous ones" painstakingly negotiated for by attrition, thanks to Uncle Abraham, had a sobering problem that should turn our heads just as much as the lascivious shenanigans going on in the twin cities: weakness and disobedience!

"Lot was the best bowler in the 'You Bet Your Life' Bowling League. For the final tournament, he bowled against the Almighty, the star player from 'The Price Is Right' League. The tournament took place at the Sodom and Gomorrah Bowling Alley and Snack Shop. Even though the lanes weren't straight and the balls were made of brimstone, the competition was fierce. First, it was down to 50 pins, then 40, then 20, then 10. The game ended abruptly when an earthquake struck, and the bowling alley caught fire. Lot grabbed two remaining pins and ran for his life, dodging falling debris and rolling brimstone balls. It was only when he was safely out in the parking lot that he discovered he'd grabbed a salt shaker as well."

As the tide of the early 1980s rolled in and out with increasingly larger and larger swells of sexual fascination, I experienced a lapping at my heels as the waves sought to engulf the self-appointed lighthouse into its rip tide as my testimony became more widely known through the rank-and-file of the department store.

George, the department store Custodian-Maintenance Man, was a likable guy. He was a husky, hulk of a fellow under his redundant, daily handyman outfit of light-blue shirt and dark-blue pants. Some days he was unshaven, complete with paint and grease stains on his hanging-too-far-below-the-belt pants and his partially untucked shirt from the day before. With a ring of keys to open every door and cabinet on planet Earth jingling at his side, he was the quintessential stereotype of a Fix-It Man.

One day, I was requested to fetch some mechanical part for a display in the Young Men's Department from the Custodial Office and Supply Room, located at the back of the third floor of the building. George's desk was at the far end of this cavernous warehouse. So, upon my arrival, I walked down the center aisle that divided the rows and rows of floor-to-ceiling shelves full of supplies for every eventual need of a cutting-edge department store.

It was also the graveyard for unused mannequins—an army of naked men, women, and children as well as adjacent shelves full of spare body parts. I walked past the vast crowds of silent dummies standing in a variety of double-jointed positions with their glassy fixed stares looking every which way. They were bathed in a bluish glow from the banks of uncovered fluorescent lights high above. My heart raced as I made the eerie trip through what looked like the props from some 1950s science-fiction thriller and onward to George's messy, vacated desk. I decided to stand there and wait for him, my written request in hand.

For a few moments, I glanced at the other three-ply requisition order forms demanding all sorts of parts and services from George and his crew that were strewn about the plateau of the desk, the Scotch-tape dispenser lying on its side next to a battered, gray stapler, the Polaroid photos of the kids and dog tacked up on the edge of the bottom shelf of the desk. As the bright white light from the desk lamp glared down from the top shelf of the desk, I absently began reading bits and pieces of the order forms when a folded-back magazine was flopped down right in front of me with a loud *smack*! Deliberately thrown into my line of vision, it was a magazine entitled *Ballin' the Jock*, and the full-size picture now in my face depicted a seemingly unnaturally well-endowed male, wearing only a T-shirt, being straddled by a woman dressed only in the same. As the act they were engaging in vaulted over the protective walls of my visual, male mind, I heard the gruff voice of George, who had quietly snuck up behind me, ask,

"What do you think of *that*, Christian Boy?"

My first and only pornographic photo took full advantage of the element of surprise and sunk its claws into the gray matter of my memory. This thought now has to be militantly taken captive time and time again, vigorously refusing to be obedient by maintaining its vivid image and seizing any opportunities to flash across my brain. George's sinister question now begs another while I wait for the transformation of the renewing of my mind:

"*Why* do you think of that, Christian Boy?"

I met a girl in the poorly attended Christian Club at the San Fernando Community College. I drank in the much-needed strength and support from the club, as I had vowed to never let happen again what had happened in my 7th-grade Science class. So, I took on any and all scientific theories, philosophies, or lifestyles adverse to my faith as they were promoted by my worldly junior-college professors and their "sycophantic" students.

I struck up a friendship with this girl, Sally Freidmann, which soon evolved into a date or two. As the relationship grew more and more serious, it became imperative that we divulge more intimate details of who we were and from where we had come. Through tears of guilt and shame, Sally confessed of being "with" a previous boyfriend that had resulted in a pregnancy and an abortion. I tried to be strong and courageous, all the while hiding my devastation. I consoled her with my own "keeping up with the Joneses" confession that I had *thought* similar things in my head, so they were also as good as committed. Hence, I am equally guilty of "offending Thee," making me eligible for the severe consequences of eye-gouging or hand-severing, as the case may be. In spite of my undaunted attempts at moving our platonic relationship forward, it was now thwarted by a frustrating chalk line of demarcation drawn down between us, dividing "thought it" from "acted upon it."

Sally eventually conceded to the dismantling of our relationship down to "just friends" with the haunting acknowledgment of her utmost desires gone awry. "Ian, you have become one of my consequences for my past, as you do not have one." I immediately retorted that I would be no such thing! How arrogant such an acceptance would be on my part. How judgmental. Now, I am a very strong proponent of that equally emphasized "going and sinning no more," but do you see me being selected to throw the first stone at the Jerusalem World Series? You can call me *anything*—"Chip Off the Old Block," "Blockhead," "Class Clown," "Christian Boy"—but do not ever call me " . . . *a consequence . . .*" Whether true or not, I cannot humanly accept that label.

I went down kicking and screaming as the relationship completely dissolved.

Colleen Branigan was a fiery Irish redhead and self-appointed atheist who wanted *nothing* to do with Christianity. In the course of our conversations during breaks between junior-college classes, it became known by my artfully subtle church-dropping that I was one of *them*! She was uncannily vicious in her extreme distaste for my faith, far more aggressive than would be anticipated, even for a strong, practicing atheist. I had not, to my knowledge, ever offended her.

Someone else had.

The previous semester, she had been run over by a believer. Spiritual road kill. Laid out bleeding and raw, flat on her back, with the "tract" marks to prove it. She recalled, with easily unearthed, intensified anger, all of the jargon, the lingo, and the cunningly luring techniques that this fisher of men had used to try to bait target Branigan. It had backfired in the dolt's face, as she had defensively parried his thrusts every time he aggressively tried to push her harder. When her obstinacy finally caved in his outreach attempts, and it was clear that she was not going to become another notch in his Four Spiritual Laws belt, he damned her to Hell and marched off to other unsuspecting fish in the sea.

I had only two semesters to try to repair the damage this village idiot had wrought. During which time, Colleen would give me the usual arguments common among all religious skeptics and atheists:

"How could your God allow wars?"

"How could He let innocent children die?"

"What about all the famine and disease in the world?"

"Where do you get off thinking that you have the only possible way to heaven?"

All to which I deliberately gave little or no response.

Ten months later, wearing my best conversational kid gloves, I had returned to my role of Toto and delicately swayed Colleen to begrudgingly admit that there *might, just might,* be the *ever so slightest* chance that this intricate, complex universe of solar and nuclear systems, web lives of plants, animals, insects, cells, DNA, molecules, seasons, stars, and planets, *might, just might possibly* have an unknown, enigmatic source with *maybe, just maybe,* a personality with intent . . .

"Look up, Colleen! Look up!"

CHAPTER THREE

Open the Door . . .

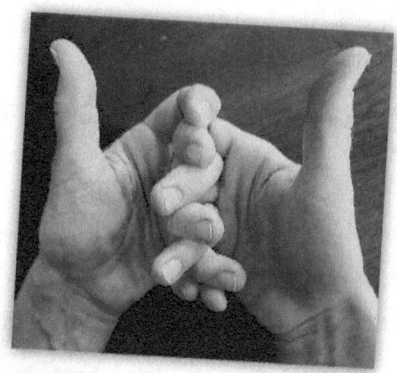

Some have called the Apostle Paul the "hinge of history," whereby he was used to swing the singular, eternal terms of Jesus over from the Jewish to the Gentile race. He was also God's commissioned instrument by which this news would travel from the far reaches of the Eastern Orient, through the doorway of the Middle East, and over the ramparts into distant, Western Europe.

Attempting to analyze and to follow this paradigm is all well and good, so long as one can appreciate the singular importance of the *hinge*.

The key is not always found in the door handle; a key can also be found in the hydraulics of the hinge.

Door movement, whether in the opening or closing, is always short-lived, as it is fraught with the time-consuming limitations enforced by the almost imperceptible descending and ascending mechanical purr of the hydraulic hinge.

The end result can either leave you entirely closed out, right where you are standing, in front of a freshly shut door—your feet firmly nailed to the floor in fear—or, the door can bump into your backside as you hesitate to walk *far enough* through the "window" of opportunity thus presented.

A life of being still and knowing He is God is filled with the sound of opening and closing doors. Hence, as foolish as this may look at times, I have tried to keep my ear to the ground, intently listening for that purring of the hydraulic hinge.

The nameplate over the first door I consciously walked through read "Ministry Opportunity."

In the circle of church life, it was nothing short of ironic that this doorway led to the newly revamped Junior Department of Our Father's Evangelical Church. Sid Barrington had retired from real estate and, childless ("*We* were his children!" he had always said), he and Esmeralda spent a majority of their weekends at a condo they had purchased in a nearby desert resort town. After many years of service, Tom and Jean Worrell were moved by the Spirit to change ministry venues and step down a rung in the chronological ladder from the Junior High Department Director-Teachers to the same position in the new 4th-, 5th-, and 6th-grade Junior Department.

I was asked to complete the trinity of rotating Sunday school teachers (Tom, Jean, Ian) for the newly combined group of students. This gave me the opportunity to practice my bulletin-honed synopses on a large group of novice converts at one time. In tribute to my ostentatious predecessor, on my first attempt, I had Jean stand by a large cassette player poised in the back of the room. I gave the anticipatory countenances in the rows of metal folding chairs fixed before me the best I could muster, suspenseful Synopsis Sid "Have I got a surprise for you!" look. I then jumped into my first—albeit deliberately-brief-to-be-compatible-with-the-nanosecond-attention-spans-of-my-charges—memorized synopsis submitted for public consumption.

> "For six days—144 hours—of trumpet-laden stalking,
> an army marches around a highly fortified city of bricks
> in great anticipation that their horns will eventually huff
> and puff and blow the house down!"

Then, like a rich tycoon sitting in the front row of an auction, I gave a subtle nod of my head in Jean's direction at the back of the room, while raising my eyebrows and flashing my eyes in assent. Jean, in turn, punched the cassette player "Play" button, which immediately blasted the room with a loud recording of blaring trumpets! The students jumped from their seats at this sudden invasion from the rear to their ears, anxiously looking around the room for the approaching, triumphant army. At another flick of my eyeballs, Jean snapped off the cassette player as I announced the invitation with great satisfaction,

"Open your Bibles, boys and girls, to the book of Joshua."

I then launched into a lesson on the curse that Joshua, while he was standing on top of a pile of bricks, bodies, and booty, had pronounced upon *anyone* who rebuilt the fallen walls of Jericho. Five hundred and twenty years later, two sons of the general contractor hired by puppet king Ahab to rebuild the walls died innocent deaths because the king did not take the time to look up the ancient curse. My application: Woe betide the person who does not gratefully respect and preserve the walls in life and relationships that God has miraculously torn down—an application I would not experience firsthand until many years to come.

However, the teacher application was *just around the corner* for me on the Sunday I gave my pupils my *Torah! Torah! Torah!* Numbers, Chapter 16 best on the *literal* pitfalls of grumbling against the leadership of God. I held up an old shoebox with a large slit in the lid and a label taped to the side reading, "Godly Complaints?"

"Upstarts Korah and Company decide that the leadership of Moses is suspect at best. They begin filling the complaint box on a daily basis with blistering opinions about the integrity of the Wilderness Administration. Moses consults the Wilderness Seismology Laboratory to seek their aid in creating a 'vacuum' of bickering. The lab technicians deliberate with the Earthly Grumbling Department of Heaven, and it is agreed that the Children of Israel should now stay clear of the Korah gang. Tents are quietly moved away from the insurrectionists during the night. At dawn, Korah emerges from his tent and fails to notice the white chalk circle around all of his family tents. He is last seen cluelessly pouring himself a cup of coffee from the kettle on the fire when he stumbles into a ditch. His comrades run to his rescue as the ditch quickly becomes larger. Soon the entire gang is seen falling into the now-gigantic, gaping cavity. Suddenly, like a clap of thunder, the earth slams shut, and someone is seen through the massive cloud of dust taking down the complaint box!"

I jumped into all manner of other ancillary ministries while continuing my sluggish academic career at the San Fernando Junior College:

I wrote my own original lesson plan for a mid-week junior-high Bible study I was teaching.

I helped chaperone that misnamed, nocturnal nightmare known as the "sleepover" at the church. Such was the extreme lassitude brought upon by partying all night long until the authorities present are dragging around with bags under their eyes and sneaking cat naps while leaning against the wall!

I drew cartoons to enhance posters plastered all around the church heralding the multitudinous events characteristic of our campus.

I sang in the college choir, which really was just an excuse for all the aspiring, non-singing comedians of the church to congregate in the back row, feigning bass, alto, tenor, or soprano capabilities in order to stick together and perform their own brand of witty subterfuge, much to the hair-pulling aggravation of the Choir Director, the Senior Pastor's wife, as she fought to make sharp all that was flat, but to no avail.

I had developed a modest keyboard talent, weaned on church haunted houses, and tried to parrot cool high-schooler "Rick" from my past as I banged away the necessary three chords on one of a fleet of battered, war-torn church pianos during the high-school morning worship hour.

I even coached a boys' T-ball team in our church league (my tribute to Owen, who was striking out opponents 3,000 miles away).

I was also asked to be a Junior High Counselor with our church for a week in the summer at the Cheyenne Christian Conference Center, a large, full-service camp facility six bus hours to the north of Monument, nestled deep within the pristine pine forests of the Sierra Nevada Mountain Range. This would be not only my first Christian camp experience, but it would also be my first extended time away from home!

Dazzling, star-studded skies, shaving cream in the sleeping bags, Bible studies, and compelling discussions late into the night, capture the flag, frogs in the girls' shower, hikes up mountains because "they're there," worship songs describing what is right outside the window, pine cones of confession thrown into the end-of-the-week bonfire, terrifying lessons on possible snake bites, frigid night swims and races in the lake, spiders and dirt everywhere you turned—my nine counselees and I experienced seven days of a great adventure unparalleled in my previous ministry experiences.

Upon my return from this highly successful "Ministry Opportunity," I pompously conjectured, "This multi-faceted, Messiah-motivated, mountaintop Mecca could really use me for longer than a mere week!"

My application for the next year's summer staff was mailed to the Cheyenne Christian Conference Center, Office of Administration, by the following February.

My concocted application was so full of myself that there was no room to doubt my being a direct blessing from God. It was banking on the lamentable premise that He was actually willing to let go of His multi-talented Ian Block from Our Father's Evangelical Church and share him with lowly camp personnel for three months in dusty, god-forsaken territory miles away from any of his *real* ministries!

The phone call from God came two months later.

"Honey!" my mom yelled to me in my bedroom. "The phone's for you!"

"Who is it?" I lazily yelled back from the horizontal position on my bed.

"I don't know, I think he said he's someone from a camp."

I rolled off the bed and shot down the hall. I was in the family room, excitedly snatching the phone from my mother, in seconds.

"Hello . . . yes, this is Ian Block . . . yes, yes, oh . . . oh, really? Well, thanks! . . . yes, okay . . . yes, um, well . . . I, uh, will have to think about it . . . uh, can I call you back . . . yeah, okay . . . yeah, . . . okay . . . thanks . . . sure—bye!"

Maintenance? They want me to do *maintenance!* The unmitigated gall of a so-called *Christian* organization to even dare to ask me to lower myself to the cleaning of bathrooms! No microphones, no pianos, no poster board—just rubber gloves and plungers! What a travesty and waste of human resources. Can you believe that?

That is exactly how I pessimistically couched my response to the inquiries from my parents about the phone call, and later to my co-workers, mentors, friends, and associates at Our Father's Evangelical Church when they asked about my plans for the upcoming summer.

God stood up, tapped his baton on the edge of the podium to get their attention, raised both arms in the air, paused for a moment for eye contact, and then directed them all to say in unison, "We think you should go!"

My Ford Mustang drove through the unwanted "Ministry Opportunity" doorway of the "Cheyenne Christian Conference Center" two months later!

Two College Department friends from our church agreed to drive up with me and bring my car back to Monument, as *I would not be needing it where I was going!*

The driveway of our home on Vista Street might as well have been the Apostle Paul's ancient dock at Miletus, as my mom, dad, brother (who was home for the summer), friends, and neighbors bid me farewell through hugs and more hugs, tears, sobbing and downright wailing and gnashing of teeth as my Mustang turned the corner and headed north, away from Ephesus, toward my hopefully potty-trained Jerusalem!

Seven hours later, my Ford Mustang "stagecoach" left the Cheyenne Christian Conference Center for the return ride back to Monument, the severed umbilical cord of all that was familiar to me trailing behind, leaving me in a dust cloud of finality.

I quickly stashed my measly luggage under the bottom mattress of one of two rickety metal bunk beds in my closet-sized, empty dorm room that was soon to be home for three other fully grown roommates for 90 long days! I rushed out of the three-story, dilapidated men's staff house that bore the awful Western name of "Boot Hill." Walking down from the knoll upon which it sat and looking back, to my gentrified mind, it vaguely resembled the house in the movie *Psycho*.

I felt my composure escaping as the reality of desperate loneliness and utter helplessness clamped around my 21-year-old soul. Frantically, I climbed up the nearest mountain I could find (to be expected, there were plenty). My body, instinctively responding to my convulsing subconscious nerves, mindlessly initiated a dismal effort to actually walk back home! But soon my defense mechanisms simultaneously saw the futility of it all and shut down in a dizzying torpor at the center of a small clearing of pine trees. All that was left of desultory Ian Block sat on a fallen log and sobbed.

Covering my face in my hands, tears pouring through the gaps in my fingers and raining down on the pine needle-blanketed dirt, I choked out in a plaintive whisper,

"O, God, what have I done? Please, God, please, God, help me! I don't know what to do. I'm scared, I'm alone—I'm so *alone.* I don't want to be here! Please, please, O, God, help me, help me!"

It was then that the manifest, undeniably supernatural comfort of the Holy Spirit of God wrapped around me to quell the sheer terror that had gripped His child.

When this peace which transcends all understanding had guarded my heart and my mind, I was able to regain a spiritual lucidity and fully absorb the reassurances thus presented:

"Ian, I've been waiting for you. I am fully aware of your glowing multi-ministry Summer Staff application. Impressive. Forget it. It is time you knew me for who *I am*, not simply vicariously through your family and church. Your position has been assured since your 3rd-grade prayer, but you have not yet seen the *power* of that position! I am the God of Abraham, Isaac, Jacob, Joseph, *and Ian!* So, let's go! Get up! Trust me."

"And the things of earth will grow strangely dim in the light of His glory and grace."

I walked down off that mountain a completely different kind of Christian from the one who'd come up it. Perhaps for the first time in my life, I had to tightly hold on to the mighty hand of God.

The Summer Staff "Round Up" Orientation took place in the massive, "whoopee ti yi yo," glass-walled (commanding an astounding view of the lake), hang 'em high-ceilinged, wagon-wheel-chandelier lit, yee-haw High School Eatin' Hall that evening.

Introductions were made around each of the fifty or so large round tables; seated Christian aliens from many different star systems sought to ease the discomfort of unfamiliarity as the feeling of being beamed down into the Wild West from the Mother Ship was pervasive.

In rotation, we newly installed "pioneers" gave our name, where we were from, and what we would be doing for the next 90 days, 2,160 hours, 129,600 minutes.

When I had finished giving my own brand of name, rank, and serial number, I could not resist an additional bemoaning of my imminent toilet-scrubbing future.

One Summer Staff returnee from the other side of the table circled the wagons around my arrow-impaled, parched soul, "Maintenance doesn't clean bathrooms, Ian. 'Accommodations' does that! You get to go around doing yard work—cutting lawns and trimming trees and raking pine needles and stuff. You do not have to clean toilets!"

Yard work? Yard work! Why, I was almost a *professional* at this! After all, it was my very first job! No cleaning bathrooms! That's the job of the poor "pardners" in "Accommodations." Yard work! What a breeze! I was beaming in my seat, relieved from the gnawing burden I had been carrying since that fateful phone call last April . . .

"My chains fell off, my heart was free, I rose, went forth, and followed . . ."

"Is there an Ian Block at this table?" I sat back down. Suddenly behind me was the voice of Annabelle Levine, wife of Camp Director Fred "Fess" (for Western effect) Levine.

"I am Ian Block!" I proudly announced, light and giddy, like a recently unleashed dog (dawg) on an endless beach!

"This is for you," responded Mrs. Levine, and she handed me a small, folded note. While all eyes around the circumference of the table were upon me, I opened the terse note and read,

Attention: Ian Block
Your work assignment is Accommodations
for the dates of June 17th.
Please report to Bob Moria on
Sunday the 17th of June, noon
Thank you . . .
Annabelle Levine
Staff Coordinator

"Saddle Up! And Move 'em out!"

Not toilets again! I had just narrowly escaped that fate! There really was a porcelain God, and He was pulling my chain! For all the while I was reading the note that *again* consigned me to everything I was *not*, the great I AM was smiling as He put the pedal to the floor and spun the Potter's wheel around a couple more times.

For the next 90 days, 2,160 hours, 129,600 minutes, I was part of a work crew: teeth-clenched smiling, non-complaining sons of Korah, who drove around the Cheyenne Christian Conference Center in beat-up, hand-me-down vans and trucks loaded down with an arsenal that could restore luster to any latrine, and daily cleaned the numerous camp bathrooms (affectionately known as "outhouses") of all the dirt and filth that could possibly be left by hundreds of kids of all ages who were away from the hygiene-enforcers at home.

On my knees, I scrubbed squeaky clean, and, on my feet, I mopped spick-and-span all the livelong day while longingly hearing the raucous laughter and competitive cheers of the camp Olympic games, the robust worship songs being belted out from the various chapels, and the ringing of the triangle "come and git it!" breakfast, lunch, and dinner "vittles" bells as they echoed through the canyons.

There I was, neighborhood suburbia colliding with Sierra Nevada, as my very own, 40-year-long wilderness experience ground on. Only my desert had two separate entrances: The nameplate over the half-moon on the one door said "MEN" and the other "WOMEN"!

The Giver of genuine humility and contentment was having His rootin', tootin' own way with pilgrim Ian as I literally plunged myself into my work!

I was sustained and fortified by the care packages and letters sent by my family and friends back in Monument, especially the weekly installments from Grandpa Colby.

He would write "religiously" every week in his usual horrible penmanship, the mundane news in and around Monument: marriages, deaths, the increasingly irritating behaviors of Grandma Melba, and the growth patterns of his lawn and shrubberies now under his solo care—a rubber-banded bundle of letters I sentimentally possess to this day.

One night, when I could not stand the "fruits and nuts" environs of the Cheyenne Christian Conference Center any longer, I cajoled Paula Henson, a fellow Accommodations staff member who was privileged to have her own car with her up at camp, to drive down the mountain to the nearest city, 90 miles straight down, so that I could kiss the pavement and see a real, live movie. So Paula and I—and her two roommates—drove down the mountain the following Saturday night.

The movie ended very late that evening, so Paula burned up the lonely highway in a desperate attempt to make the Cheyenne Christian Conference Center's strict curfew. An unsuspecting rabbit did not know that we were so pressed for time and decided that there was, in fact, enough distance between our front fender and his fluffy brown tail to dart across the otherwise deserted two lanes stretched out in front of him and safely skirt under the guard rail in front of the bushy embankment on the other side. Peter Cottontail did not know what hit him as Paula plowed right over the scurrying creature. The bunny was big enough to create a "speed bump" sensation for the sitting occupants of Paula's careening Volkswagen Beetle as the tire catapulted Bugs from under the chassis to that great carrot patch in the sky.

Paula slammed on her brakes and stared into the rearview mirror. Her animal-loving personality was heartbroken as she caught a glimpse of the inert ball of fur hugging one of the intermittent white reflectors that dotted the center of the highway.

I could not help but think of atheist Colleen Branigan just then, and her hit-and-run experience with a near-fatal, pedestrian-proselytizing gospel, but my reverie was jolted by the sound of the driver's side door being opened and Paula racing back down the road to see if there was any hope for Thumper. The three of us left in the Beetle could not help howling with laughter as we turned around to view the sight of Paula standing in the middle of the highway, in the dark of night, stooped down, longingly hovering over the dead rabbit, waiting for it to somehow hop up into her arms.

Fortunately, Paula, too, finally saw the dark humor of it all, and we laughed all the way back up the mountain and even while sneaking back into our respective dorms well after curfew.

The next morning, I taped a sign on the door of Paula's dorm, "Home of the Rabbit Killer!" I even went so far as to have a new Cheyenne Christian Conference Center badge made for her that also read, "Rabbit Killer." I assumed the role of Class Clown for a third time in my life and continued perpetuating the humorous, murderous nickname for Paula Henson among the entire staff throughout the balance of the summer. I had failed to check all of this with the great C.P.A. in the sky, Who would one day peruse the Galatian General Journal looking at my life's debits and credits that would give an account of all my sowing and reaping.

One afternoon during the final week of the summer, I was in another dorm room down the hall from my own, talking to fellow staff members (I was now familiar, to varying degrees of friendships, with all of the male inhabitants of "Boot Hill"— although some really did belong in the *Psycho* house!) about our plans for the Fall. One of the camp dishwashers handed me a catalogue that had been lying on his bunk bed as testimony of his upcoming aspirations. The cover depicted a beautiful photo of an enticing college campus and bore the title "Antioch Christian Academy 1979/1980." I thumbed through the pages, enchanted with the novel idea of an accredited, liberal-arts Christian education. It was down in Orange County, an area some 40 miles south of Monument, so named for the California citrus fruit that, at one time, dominated these flat lands with rows and rows of trees. I put the catalogue back on the bed, put my spiritual ear to the ground, and listened for the possible sound of an opening hydraulic hinge to higher education.

My own private stagecoach, with my dad driving and my mom riding shotgun, picked me up from the Cheyenne Christian Conference Center in September.

Immediately upon my arrival back in Monument, I made a beeline for the home of Colby and Melba Block. When I opened their front door, my surprised and elated grandparents sprang from their individually designed Mama Bear and Papa Bear rocking chairs in an amazingly incongruous display of twilight-years adrenaline as I ran up to hug their frail frames!

A truly changed man was now back home from his wonderful mountaintop experience. But it was not long before I was back in the head-banging trenches of the San Fernando Junior College, plowing through another world-battling semester against the big guns mounted on the think tanks of higher learning.

I felt like David soon after the toppling-of-Goliath victory parties, who found himself sequestered from friends and family alike, all alone in a cave in Adullam, writing the elegiac psalms of a spelunker to the sound of dripping stalactites.

It was then that my heart heard the door closing at the San Fernando Junior College, and I asked my parents early on in the throes of the Fall semester if I could transfer to the Antioch

Christian Academy in the Spring. I could hear the anticipated hydraulic hinge purring open as they both enthusiastically nodded their heads.

Our Vista Street driveway now became the old Port of Caesarea as I drove my mileage-accumulated Mustang down to the orange groves of Rome and through the doorway marked, "Antioch Christian Academy."

As if they had sequentially finished their earthly tasks pertaining to their investment in me, my beloved grandparents uncannily began to be called to their eternal home in cruel succession soon after I was entrenched in dorm life and studies at the Antioch Christian Academy. I was not even able to attend the first funeral of my Grandfather Carl in the Spring of 1980, as his untimely death occurred during the intense intellectual heat of finals.

Like instinctively communicating dominoes, both my Grandmothers Frances and Melba passed away only four months apart, during the following Summer and Fall, for completely different health reasons. Their funerals were moving testimonies of fighting good fights and finishing races. My Lois and Lois were buried next to Grandpa Carl at the verdant Monument Memorial Park and Gardens in the hills east of town. I thank my God every time I remember them: the sleepovers, the lunches and dinners out, the delightful weekend excursions (especially that time so etched in satisfaction when I was blissfully paroled from my 4th-grade curriculum and boarded ship for a four-day adventure on exotic Catalina Island—one elated grandson—the sole guest of honor to all four of his devoted grandparents), and above all, the salient conversations about their lives as they intertwined with mine, and guided me like waving red flashlights down the runway of my childhood.

The common phone rang in the hallway of my dorm at the Antioch Christian Academy the following December, and I already had a dark premonition as to its possible recipient and message, as Grandfather Colby had been in and out of the hospital for many months and had been reported as not doing very well. Like a series of stormy waves slapping up against me, I splashed around looking for calmer waters. I found none as I picked up the hall phone after my name, as drearily predicted by my pounding heart, had been called. It was Owen, uncharacteristically somber and obviously shaken. "Ian," he said, "you'd better drive up here as soon as you can. Grandpa (sadly, he no longer needed to specify which one) is not doing well and, well, the doctors don't have much hope."

I slammed closed my books in an apathetic disregard for more heady, puffed-up knowledge and jumped into my car, recklessly speeding northward toward Monument, bent on holding on to what really mattered in life for as long as I could grasp it.

There is no place more festive and beautiful than Monument, California, at Christmas time. It was a shame that the circumstances pulling me back into town during the holiday season of 1980 were not more joyful, joyful.

Monument is an enviable, odd oasis. In the arid, tract-home, tilt-up utilitarian commercial and industrial buildings that provided the framework for the typical Southern California cities and towns endlessly sprawling with a regretful lack of distinction, Monument is a unique nucleus.

But it is surrounded by the slipshod and spontaneous. Stereotypical claim-stake communities cropped up like movie props in unison with the likewise burgeoning television and movie industries propelling them. Unlike the enclaves of palatial estates of the very, very few who made it big, these conventional habitats seemed to suddenly appear overnight to house the supporting work force of the industry—not unlike the shanty towns of old, those brainchildren of money-making schemers in response to the flood of demands consequential to the infiltration and explosions of megalomaniacal populations who swarmed to California or Alaska in madcap rushes for gold.

However, would-be builders and developers who migrated specifically to Monument, California, on the heels of some Hollywood dream, were obligated to fall into step architecturally. Their blueprint was our own City Hall—a Victorian-style flagship, complete with turrets and intricate corbels. Even later commercial construction (with growth severely restricted by our sage City Council) submitted to this symbolic ultimatum to conform and were creatively built to the same Victorian specifications.

To top it off, Valentino Avenue also sported double-lighted Victorian lampposts, supporting colorful baskets of blooming seasonal flowers. These illuminated both sides of the street up the entire length of the hill, across Main Street, to the top at Ridgeway Avenue.

Quaint shops and businesses spanned both sides of the ascending boulevard with tangential streets and cul-de-sacs providing access to equally inviting neighborhoods of uniquely English Tudor, French Normandy, Bavarian, Victorian, Spanish, or Mediterranean homes of myriad sizes and shapes.

When Christmas lights are strung across Valentino Avenue (with all of the adjacent houses joining in on the decorative frenzy), and the large wreath is lit on Our Father's Evangelical Church's steeple at the top of the hill, Monument, California, rivals the most picturesque alpine ski resort in Colorado. The only difference was that *our* advanced slope was the actual bridge of a broken-off, red spray-painted nose!

The only eyesore that was crammed into the freeway view of our town was that of Monument Hospital. It was manufactured with modern expedience as a pressing civic necessity for the health and well-being of the citizenry. Situated adjacent to the English Tudor Monument Museum (which *did* conform to the whole), the hospital was a futuristic monstrosity snuck in at the bottom of the hill. A shiny, aluminum ugly duckling amidst the conforming gables, dormers, beveled glass, and tapering chimneys of the surrounding swans.

It was into the multi-level parking lot of this brazen behemoth that I drove, as this was the sterile laboratory into which my grandfather had been incarcerated for terminal illness. I made my way through the labyrinthine hallways of the valley of the shadow of death until I came to Room #209, a private, synthetic, cell-block cubicle. Behind the plastic curtain hung from an oval track in the ceiling, propped up to a comfortable conversational setting by the mechanical hospital bed, lay my grandfather, who, somehow, was expecting to see me. I tried to conceal the startled look on my face, as first sight had revealed a ghastly decline in Colby Block. The light blue, tie-in-the-back hospital gown had replaced the faded Levis and patched flannel shirts, a bare head his cowboy hat, and removed false teeth allowed his cheeks to invert to fill in the new cavity, creating a gaunt face and causing a slurred-speech impediment. Regardless, the emaciated shell was *still* my grandfather.

"Pull up a chair, Ian, and sit for a spell," he slurred.

I obeyed.

My family had slipped down to the hospital cafeteria for dinner, so we were alone. He slur-yelled to the nurse at her station outside his door to get us a can of 7-Up and two plastic glasses.

As we drank, he asked about college, wanting to make sure that they (whoever *they* were) were treating me well or "heads are gonna roll!" I am not sure what sort of temple cleansing he would have been able to whip up from the confines of his hospital bed with his nostrils connected to oxygen tubes, but he was nonetheless convinced he could call up a posse if I so much as said the word. I asked the expected "How are you feeling?" not wanting to know the real answer. He must have sensed this perfunctory question for what it was and gave me what I asked for, a safely pat, "Fine, just fine."

Our conversation was brief, as he quickly grew tired, and measured, as if we were meeting each other for the very first time. Yet underneath our surface banter was a gut-wrenching, deeply profound dialogue going on between grandfather and grandson that spoke volumes of the years we had shared together, as well as the unequivocal terms of finality unafraid to rear its ugly head and admit that this was the last conversation we would ever have together.

I stood to go. I stared at him for a minute, as I thought he had dropped off to sleep, and I could savor what I knew in my heart was a moment with eternity breathing down our necks. Before my emotions got the best of me, I walked out of the doorway. A few steps down the hall, I heard behind me, under breath expelled with obvious effort, "Goodbye, Ian."

"Good-bye, Grandpa," I half-whispered to myself before I started sobbing.

From the top level of the parking lot of the Monument Hospital, if it had not been in the dark of oncoming Winter, I would have been able to notice a lightning-shaped fissure that had formed while I was away at college down the left side of Rudolph Valentino's face—from the front of his left ear, traversing in jagged exploration down the left side of his nose, and separating his confident lips and jutting jaw. The glacial regimens of Father Time were inexorably marching onward.

The iconoclastic patriarch of the Block family left this Earth two days later, two weeks before Christmas. I am no longer a restful, merry gentleman when the holidays roll around. They are now tainted with "loved-one loss." My whole family feels this pall each in their own way. Over the years, I have tried to let nothing dismay me, fitfully trying to remember the good tidings that Christ our Savior was born on Christmas day to save us all from Satan's power when we were gone astray. I am mindful that my defense against demons is in part due to my past relationships with my four grandparents, particularly Colby Block, whose mere presence, without speaking a word, exemplified the Rock of Ages.

Grandpa Colby's funeral was a largely attended, civic event. The crowds of mourners and well-wishers covered the hills of the Monument Memorial Park and Gardens. My family and I were approached by countless clients, business associates, members of our church, and even elderly ex-deacons who had been present during that last famous deacon meeting when my grandfather had walked out. Widowed Doris Mackintosh even made it to the graveside, supporting herself with a wooden cane. I could barely hear the condolences in my numbed, melancholic, bereaved state as people came up and either hugged me or shook my hand. But a common theme ran throughout their remarks: "Your grandfather was one of the most giving, honest men I ever knew."

After his funeral, and arriving back at the Antioch Christian Academy, I shut my car door and walked across the parking lot to my dorm with tears, sorrows like sea billows, rolling down my face. My imagination had become frightfully aware the moment my car door had slammed shut that the nameplate over the door that had just banged into my backside from the insensitive recoiling of the hydraulic hinge read,

"End of an Era."

CHAPTER FOUR

There's All the People . . .

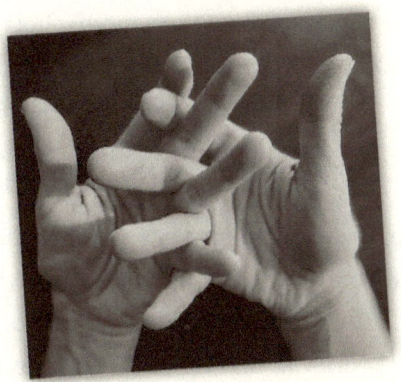

Charles Dickens begins his classic, *David Copperfield*, with the following words,

> "Whether I shall turn out to be the hero of my own life,
> Or whether that station will be held by anybody else,
> These pages must show."

One can look back on his life to the many seasons of sustained fortitude, as well as moments of sheer victories over the darkness, and be able to credit these to the specific contributions of a broad compilation of unsung heroes investing in him over a lifetime.

They will have come in all shapes and sizes, ages, and abilities. Their heroic acts are equally as varied. Most efforts are quiet and nondescript, while some deeds can attract attention and the clamoring of autograph hounds as they surround the recipient, seeking an audience with this new celebrity.

Usually, the genuine unsung hero does not want their name in the paper, an interview on television, or a human-interest plug on the radio. It is enough for them that the *object* of their heroics has been protected or has succeeded. This is as it should be.

But the direct recipients of these heroic acts, if they are not fools, know *exactly* who the real heroes are in their lives. And, more often than not, these quiet heroes are not the ones currently surrounded, with everyone pointing and exclaiming, "Look at all the people!"

Antioch Christian Academy is so named because it is surrounded. Its first-century Syrian namesake was the birth mother of the Gentile Church. This burgeoning body of Christ was not fostered in some primeval, marble-hewn dust bowl, as some have misconceived Bible times, but rather it was a highly advanced, cosmopolitan city—the third largest in the known world of its day and the third most influential in the Roman Empire.

Antioch boasted its own advancements for the hedonistic sake of its aristocratic, wealthy inhabitants. Everything from world-renowned, high-bred racehorses for their "Ben Hur" chariot competitions, to an advanced system of citywide floodlighting for all-night entertainment.

Houses with central heating, indoor plumbing, and swimming pools. Multiple theaters, bath houses, fountains, thousands of marble columns, ornate temples, and large marketplaces. They even prided themselves on a four-and-one-half-mile-long main street that divided chariot and horse traffic down the center from pedestrian traffic on either side, all under the skies of one of the finest climates in the world.

It is here that the Gentile Church cut against the grain of the surrounding society, and it is in Orange County that the modern-day Antioch Christian Academy became a highly respected, faith-based enclave, in the midst of the entertainment capital of the world.

Not only did this institution provide me with the very well-rounded, biblical education I was starving for, it also served as the venue in which I would stretch myself into a larger social sphere, as the college attracted students from all over the world. My paltry 40-mile drive south from Monument, California, paled in comparison to the globetrotting performed by a large segment of the student body.

As I had already spent quite some time at the San Fernando Junior College endeavoring to put General Education under my scholastic belt, I was able to transfer to the Antioch Christian Academy as a junior. My affable roommate, first by assignment and then by mutual choice, for the duration of the next two years, was sophomore Malcolm Davis.

He had already settled into our room on the second floor of the men's dormitory and was lying on his back on his bed when I arrived with suitcases, duffle bag, and various and sundry boxes of what I thought would be extremely important educational supplies. I attempted to jam my way through the doorway carrying everything at once and was permanently wedged in within seconds.

Malcolm looked up from his pillow, his arms behind his head, and casually said his first words to me, "Do you *always* do everything all at once?" He smiled as he slid off the bed and helped pry me loose from my ill-fated attempt.

"Hi!" he said, shaking my hand. "I'm Malcolm Davis. You must be Ian Block?"

"Yeah." I replied, slightly out of breath from my can-opener experience. "Nice to meet you, Malcolm."

I threw the bulk of my gear on my side of the room, making it look instantly like the bed of the Joad truck from *The Grapes of Wrath*. I decided to put off the sorting and moving-in ritual for a minute and chat with this new acquaintance of mine. He was somewhat shorter than me (which was no surprise, as I was quite tall by then), with a very slender waistline contrasted with a buffed-up upper body, including the bulging pectorals that result from frequent encounters with a weight room. He had an electric smile that made his entire face beam and a gold-cross earring pierced through one ear lobe. He was also black.

I sensed early on that we could have a close, "iron sharpening iron" relationship with the proper investment of time and a good dose of open-mindedness. During the infancy stages of our friendship, while we two territorial males were jockeying for position, assessing and reassessing each other's moves and motivations, I noticed, from time to time, the inevitable issue of race would crop up like the tire spikes in a parking-lot driveway keeping you out of an exit.

I misconstrued this invisible defense shield of Malcolm's to be some sort of chip on his shoulder, and, instinctively, my first inclination was to ignorantly push the chip right off his back by using what in the original, inerrant manuscripts were divinely powerful division-wrecking-ball proclamations, "One faith, one Lord, one baptism," ". . . neither Jew nor Greek, slave or free," ". . . Christ is all and in all." But coming through the oral filters of tall, blonde, white boy Ian Block from cute little upper middle-class Monument, California, it sounded more like a trite, manufactured "hurry up and get over it" attempt at spiritual detente. It was all a subcutaneous irritant to Malcolm, and rightly so, as the color of his skin would still remain after my sorry attempt at unifying bait from the Bible. It all crumbled to the floor immediately after my saying it, forming a pile of well-intentioned word dust that quickly scattered to the four winds under the gale of his ancestors' visceral heritage.

These racial walls, when they were erected, would only come down brick by brick, as the Father seemed to want us *both* to engage in the arduous process of doing so from both of our heel-dug positions. A miraculous Jericho pulverization was apparently *not* the correct learning experience here. That sort of instantaneous breakthrough would happen later in my life.

Over the next few months, through the turmoil and travails of college life—girlfriends, finals, food fights, dorm-room pranks, chapel, pop quizzes, athletic events, all-night study parties—Malcolm and I carved out a very enduring friendship. As we grew closer, we were able to respectfully recognize a racial impasse when we saw one coming. We even became so familiar with the warning signs that we came to smile through the inevitable "There will be no walking in the other's moccasins today!" Confident that one day *that* brick, too, would be removed, and that, in the meantime, it was not mandatory. Until then, we were like two stone masons at the work site of the Tower of Babel, who, in split-second mid-chisel, are suddenly incapable of fully comprehending one another.

"A church 'Expansion for Ministry' project goes awry when the Worship Center is constructed taller than the blueprints allowed. Since the Design Review Board did not consult with the Engineer to draw up the plans in the first place, He abruptly halts the project by changing the languages of the contractors and subcontractors into individual jargon that puts a strain on their terminology tool belts. The building project is permanently scrapped because the Foreign Language Program immediately created to alleviate the problem cannot handle the class size."

Yet we both learned to be awed and appreciative of what God was doing in our unique friendship. It was that same feeling of wonderment, reminiscent of one's salvation experience and a lack of fully grasping the depth of love initiated on our behalf.

We did not completely understand where each of us had come from, but we knew where we would like to go. The bottom line in the interim was that we were becoming the best of friends, and Jonathan did not care about the color of David's skin or vice versa. I grew to really like Malcolm, love him, and he me.

I visited his family where they lived in Los Angeles, and he came up to Monument to meet mine. Not since the Four Musketeer days did I feel such an affinity with this man of another race and color. Although, a brand-new Four Musketeers would have a brief theatrical renaissance shortly.

Our Father's Evangelical Church was too great a distance for me to traverse every Sunday morning. I found that many at the Antioch Christian Academy involved themselves in the gargantuan First Congregational Church just a few miles from our campus. It was not long before I was neck-deep by habit in weekend ministries at this very large church that could swallow Our Father's Evangelical whole!

Malcolm and I joined the college choir and drama team just in time for their Spring production, *In Him Was Life*. It was a musical extravaganza depicting the life of Christ as narrated by the four good-news authors, Matthew, Mark, Luke, and

John. Choirs, featuring small musical ensembles, full orchestra, Christian "choreography"(dancing!), and special effects!

Malcolm was hesitant to try out for one of the four lead parts. He was a Chemistry major with a more behind-the-scenes personality. I, the Speech Communications major with a minor in Biblical Education, could not wait for the chance of auditioning.

The largest of the speaking parts was that of Matthew, which, to no one's surprise, I nabbed on the basis of my out-standing thespian capabilities. Malcolm was awarded the role of John. I consoled his trepidation by offering him my personal drama coaching right in the convenience of our own dorm room! Another student whom I did not know from the Antioch Christian Academy was to play Luke, Trent Farrell. The last part, Mark, went to a student from the local State College who had attended First Congregational for quite some time, Santiago Alvarez.

It was a vigorous rehearsal schedule that intensified as the one-night performance drew nearer. I coached Malcolm on the art of diction, articulation, projection, and stage presence—the master of speech tutoring the aspiring chemist.

Dress rehearsals at the church were exhilarating for me as I looked around the cavernous 7,000-seat Worship Center, picturing it with standing room only on the evening of the per-formance. I thought I was a Director's dream as I strutted about the platform, preening like a peacock with the knowledge that I was indeed the Socrates who could salvage these embryonic orators. However, there was some irreverent grumbling when I offered too many brilliant staging suggestions to the Director, and a running joke ensued behind my back that "No matter how hard you try, you still can't block, Block!"

The night to remember was soon upon us. Malcolm, Trent, and Santiago were terrified as we looked out from the wings backstage to see exactly what I had dreamt of: thousands of people jammed into the pews, with standing room only. Trent whispered in awe as he stared into the auditorium, "Look at all the people!"

Before we knew it, the lights had dimmed, the crowd had hushed, and the Music Director took to his platform, baton in hand, to commence the overture. *In Him Was Life* had begun!

For the next two hours, the new, live onstage version of D' Artagnan, Athos, Porthos, and Aramis traded in their swords and shields for robes and tunics as we embodied Matthew, Mark, Luke, and John. I stood up to open the pageant; as the spotlight flashed into my eyes, the sea of people riveted on me were no longer visible. With a sweeping gesture of my arms, I began,

"Hello, my name is Matthew, the Tax Collector, and I want to tell you a story of . . ."

I was flawless. Surprisingly, as the play progressed, so were Malcolm, Trent, and Santiago—surely due in part to my supreme coaching throughout the rehearsals. I soaked up the limelight like a sponge as more than 7,000 people hinged on my every word.

The musical had some very interesting "play within a play" scenes, in which one of the four principals would play *other* roles in The Greatest Story Ever Told. One of these was the 40-day temptation of Jesus in the Wilderness. Matthew would set up the scene and then role-play Jesus famished in the desert, as Santiago's Mark would play the part of Satan. Under a bank of eerie red spotlights, Santiago channeled the most serpentine, diabolical, Spanish Inquisition Satan I had ever seen as he crouched down and darted in and out of the space surrounding my kneeling Jesus and hissed out the first of his dares,

"If you are the Son of God, tell this stone to become bread!"

I looked up at Santiago with divine defiance blazing in my eyes and, with all the pathos I could muster, screamed into his face,

"IT IS WRITTEN: MAN DOES NOT LIVE ON BREAD ALONE!"

I put my head back down as the audience sat bolt-upright in suspenseful anticipation of Satan's next move. I was smugly convinced that our Temptation in the Wilderness reenactment was better than the original!

The Father sat back in His plush, heavenly reclining chair, feet propped up on a cushy footstool shaped like planet earth, a blazing fire in the eye-shaped hearth. He thumbed through the pages of His Holy Word, muttering as he searched, "Ian . . . Ian . . . Ian . . . Ah—here we are!," He exclaimed in satisfaction. He read to Himself a few words from the *real* Jesus, as recorded by the *real* Tax Collector, "He who exalts himself shall be . . ." He instantly looked up from the page to His Son, who was standing in the doorway, waiting, and gave an assenting nod of His head. The Son nodded in return, perfectly perceiving the task at hand—and instantly vanished . . .

"I will give you all authority and splendor, for it has been given to me, and I can give it to anyone I want to. So if you worship me, it will be all yours!"

I looked up at Santiago's villainous face after he had finished this second enticement. Then I sighed in a very effective pregnant pause before I stood from my kneeling position, towering over short Santiago, and pointed into his evil face. It was in that moment in eternity that some divine agent deliberately crossed the wires of my perfectly memorized script, mixing the next two scriptural responses from Jesus ("Thou shalt love the Lord thy God and Him only!" and "Thou shalt not put the Lord thy God to a foolish test!") into one grandiose theological error. It was hard to miss, for it was again screamed for dramatic effect . . .

"THOU SHALT NOT LOVE THE LORD THY GOD!"

Satan melted in horror at this unexpected new version of the Gospels. His face transformed from Nemesis From Hell to helpless, stunned, wide-eyed shock, which said, in out-of-character anguish, "Ian, what have you done?" There was an audible gasp that rippled through the massive audience of the mega-church as people put fingers in their ears, drilling for a possible wax obstruction as they looked at each other and asked, "Did I hear that correctly—did Jesus just deny the Father?"

Mark, Luke, John, and *the Blasphemer* limped through the rest of the musical in spite of the cloud that now hovered over it in mocking recognition that it was now impossible to achieve dramatic perfection as a result of the very one supposedly most *unlikely* to blow it.

The cast party after the production was stigmatized. The congratulatory remarks all around were half-hearted; the wind had been knocked out of everyone's sails. I went to bed that night in my dorm room ashamed of my arrogance and shaken by the consequences.

I woke up the next morning and noticed a humorous sign written by some clown on our dorm floor taped to my door as I went out for breakfast, "Home of the Heretic!" I later discovered that the sign artist was none other than my dishwasher friend from the Cheyenne Christian Conference Center, who not only had a very good memory but was still very good friends with Paula Henson! Rejoice, "Rabbit Killers," Farmer Block has just reaped his comeuppance!

In compensation for my waywardness, I dove into my studies like never before. Only this time, it was not for the applause of men. I was humbly studying, writing essays, debating, and speechmaking for an audience of *One*. I had learned a big lesson the hard way in direct proportion to the previous size of my head. I was determined never to let that happen again. Direct from the jaws of speechmaking Job, "The Lord had given, and the Lord had taken away." So now my talents and gifts were no longer displayed for personal exhibition purposes but would now be a steeple on top of my temple of the Holy Spirit, encouraging and admonishing people to once again, "Look up!"

However, my academic diligence did pay off in the "applause from men" department as I was able to graduate *cum laude* as well as receive the most Outstanding Student Award from the Speech Communications Department of the Antioch Christian Academy. With these accolades bolstering me, I entertained all sorts of future career possibilities, everything from full-time ministry, to public-school teaching, to continuing with postgraduate education and obtaining a Master's degree or more. I could not distinguish one hydraulic-hinge sound from the other, so I invited my father and mother down to Orange County, shortly before my graduation, to pick their brains regarding their youngest son and to help sort things out.

We went out to dinner at a local Mexican restaurant, and I posed the question to them after prefacing my remarks with all of the plaudits I was receiving from my soon-to-be alma mater. My father and mother listened patiently.

Then my father said in response to my aspirations about obtaining a Master's degree, "Why would you want to do that, Ian? The ink's not even dry on your first degree. Why don't you use it first and then see if you need another one?"

The essence of the conversation distilled down to the "family business." In 1927, Colby Block had started an Insurance Agency in Monument. My father had taken over the business at the time of Grandpa Colby's retirement, and the search was on for the next chip off the old Block!

I was the logical choice, as Owen had since graduated and was back in California, working as a coach at a college in Los Angeles. He had no interest in pushing paper; he would much rather put a shot. I, too, had my share of ambivalence regarding the family business. True, it had provided us a marvelous life, with Seth Block home at decent hours and able to attend all of our sporting events and school plays. It just did not entice me, as it seemed *I* was selling myself short. But my father was not yet done with *his* bit of selling.

"You know, Ian, your mother and I have watched you in all of your ministries at O.F.E. (acronymic deacon slang for our church), and working in the family business would allow you plenty of free time to carry on with those ministries at the church."

I had to let that one simmer. It was indeed a compelling argument. I could fuse both my Communications and Bible degrees into a ministry at the church, using my job as a means to that end. It was a complete turnaround in perspective from the all-encompassing career obsessions of the new workaholics pouring out of college campuses in the early 1980s, but it was a unique opportunity, to be seriously weighed at any rate. I still cringed at the thought of becoming another Jim Anderson, the insurance agent from T.V.'s *Father Knows Best*, even though I was destined to have my very own "Princess" and "Kitten" soon!

The conversation soon digressed into potential graduation presents. I told my parents I would really like an *experience* instead of a material gift. My parents were in part the cause of this wanderlust in me, as they had dragged Owen and me on many a trailer-hauling summer road trip until we had seen every monument, historical site, cave, natural formation, and National Park in the continental United States: The Everglades, Niagara Falls, New Orleans' French Quarter, Devil's Tower, Great Sand Dunes, Independence Hall, the Liberty Bell. We saw the homes of Washington, Jefferson, and Lincoln, as well as their likenesses on our city's inspiration, Mount Rushmore. We were also yelled at by Park Rangers, chased by bears, spit on by geysers, stranded on a Canadian glacier in a broken-down snowmobile tractor, ducking darting bats swarming out of Carlsbad Caverns, involuntarily swimming with sharks on a sandbar in the Gulf Coast of Florida, as well as capsizing our canoe in the turgid, snake-infested waters of the appropriately named Blackwater River in the swampy Sunshine State. My parents were under the noble impression that this would assist in properly coloring our educational experience, and they were patently correct!

One of these educational experiences occurred at a stopover in Yellowstone National Park. My father wanted to create an ultimate male bonding experience with his boys, so we left my mother at the trailer one day and drove to the shores of Lake Yellowstone for an afternoon of trout fishing. None of us had had much experience or interest in fishing, but it looked like just the thing to do for boys to become men or vice versa.

So we each sat by the lakeside and cast our lines into the beautiful, placid waters of Lake Yellowstone. Trout fishing had a bit more action attached to it than the usual sedentary fishing experience. You must keep casting and reeling in your line in order for the lure to create the illusion of live bait for the fish. Our immediate quarry would not be duped by the usual writhing worm on a stationary hook.

So, like an adopted son of the Zebedee clan, I cast and reeled, cast and reeled, cast and reeled, waiting for a bite. The trout were too smart that day and were not to be fooled by the fabricated moving meal that skirted past them at predictable intervals. Still, I mindlessly flicked my fishing pole, shooting the lure further and further out into the waters of the lake; then I would turn the crank yet again, bringing the ignored bait back to shore.

Owen and my father were on either side of me, each quite a few yards down the path that hugged the shoreline. They, too, were casting and reeling, casting and reeling in robotic fever, like two gambling addicts endlessly pulling on slot-machine levers.

We were not doing much in the way of conversation that afternoon. Not until I finally caught something!

It was like any other of the previous hundred casting exercises, only this time, the effect was unique. There was no tugging on my pole, no splashing death dance of the scaly catch at the end of my line. In fact, there had been no splash at all! After casting my line as far as I could send it, my lure had mysteriously made no entrance into the water.

I thought that maybe I had missed it in my bored state, or perhaps it was due to the sun's glare on the shimmering water. I began reeling in my line. As the reel rolled up the fishing line, the final destination of the lure became more apparent. I continued cranking, following the line right out of the water, up onto the dirt, and around behind my back! It was then that a cold sweat began to gel on my forehead. I continued cranking until the line was taut on my pole and I could feel the pull at the other end . . . in my neck!

In a panic, I called to my father, who came running. He discovered that the three-pronged fish hook had lodged itself into the back of my head! No wonder there was no splash! I had cast out and caught myself!

While Owen laughed uproariously, my father took out a pair of cutters and wisely cut off the lure and line, and clipped off the exposed two barbs of the fish hook. It was impossible to dislodge the remaining barb. I began to cry. Owen continued to laugh, although more discreet under the scolding eye of my father.

So much for our male bonding!

We quickly gathered up our fishing gear and sped to the local Yellowstone Hospital. A very experienced doctor escorted me into an examination room and reassured my father that fish-hook accidents are quite common and that he performed all kinds of extractions on a daily basis.

After a brief dose of local anesthetic, while I clenched my teeth, the doctor took a pair of pliers and expertly re-routed the embedded fish hook back the way it had come. With the hook remains still clamped between his pliers, and while I felt the first tingles of fainting, the doctor said to my father that the hook had in fact slipped upwards under the layers of the skin at the back of my neck and came to rest underneath the base of my skull. It could only have been removed "professionally."

While we drove back to our campsite, with Owen salivating over the embellished tale he would try to tell our mother, I commiserated in the back seat. I had taken Jesus' invitation to become a fisher of men to a whole new level that day! It's a good thing that the fishing method back in those disciple-gathering days was only nets. If not, I am sure Doctor Luke could have kept up a thriving side practice of removing hooks out of new converts!

Antioch Christian Academy sent a group of interested students over to Europe every June, and I wanted to tag along this year. My parents agreed that this would be a wonderful graduation-gift idea. So, after the ceremony, I was whisked off to the airport. Like Jimmy Stewart's George Bailey in *It's a Wonderful Life*, I was doing everything possible to see the world and avoid settling back down in my sleepy little hometown. So I had joined a group of fellow students for a six-week exploration of Europe!

England, Scotland, Germany, Switzerland, Italy. Buckingham Palace, the canals of Venice, the Matterhorn, the Coliseum. It was a whirlwind experience that was awe-inspiring! I was particularly moved when I deliberately lagged behind our tour deep within the catacombs under Rome as the others began heading topside. I received a taste of the foreboding dread and darkness that was both this graveyard of saints and birthplace of the secret fish symbol. It was only a few moments of solitude, but it connected me with the tumultuous past of Christianity's Founding Fathers, sitting there in the blackness with their families and friends as clods of dirt fell on top of them from the tunnel ceiling above, the result of the pounding, searching armies overhead.

Belgium, Wales, Austria, France. My first sight of the Eiffel Tower was breath-taking! As I explored the levels of this Erector Set final exam of 1889, I noticed that a brand-new restaurant was being constructed on the second level that overlooked the vast rectangular fountains leading up to Trocadero Square. Had it not been a gridiron floor, I might have been able to put my ear to the ground and hear the sound of a future hydraulic hinge.

But before I knew it, the trip was over, and I was back in my bedroom on Vista Street. In a flash, I found myself wearing a shirt and tie from nine to five, sitting behind a desk on the second floor of the English Tudor small-business building off Valentino Avenue, looking out of the corner window at Rudolph's distant, cracking face, picking up the constantly ringing phone and cheerfully saying, "Good morning, Block Insurance!"

I grew up with Maria Ponticelli. As a matter of fact, she actually remembers the time Glen Tollockson and I deliberately sat on *her* side of the 2nd-grade Department as I, unknowingly, sat next to her!! She had shaken her head in imperial disgust at this immature antic from the "frog, snail, puppy-dog tail" concoction verifying God's profound sense of humor. I guess the long-term joke was on Maria if she had known it—she was then sitting next to her future husband!

The Ponticellis had moved to California from upstate New York when Maria was a baby. They settled in Monument in 1961, and her father, Paulo Ponticelli, started a business as a contractor. They began attending Our Father's Evangelical Church shortly thereafter.

She had begun admiring the awkward, blond Ian Block from afar for many years after our first embarrassing, delinquent-behavior encounter. We became better friends as the years wore on. She even remembers a pang of jealousy at the infamous Junior High Christmas party "Choo-Choo" game that night at the Worrells' when I was kissing Tammy Wyngate. She was far to the front of the line, just behind the coal car but nonetheless had kept her "green eyes" on my caboose.

When I came back into town after my graduation trip to Europe, I saw Maria at church the following Sunday. She was beautiful. After the rocky romances of my San Fernando Junior

College days, and the pitiful attempts made at the Antioch Christian Academy, Maria Ponticelli was a breath of fresh air. With the rock-solid foundation of a childhood friendship, and her, to my amazement, not dating anyone at the time, our friendship glided into something far more serious within the first few months of my arrival back in Monument.

I was smitten by this gorgeous Italian, probably much the same as Sid Barrington was smitten by Esmeralda so many years earlier. I knew I was madly in love by the following Christmas and began planning a most extravagant engagement.

I called Malcolm Davis at the Antioch Christian Academy, who was in his last semester before graduation. I asked if the school was still planning to take students to Europe again this year. He said "Yes." I then told him of my wild and crazy idea.

I broached the subject of traveling to Europe with Maria, that it might be good for her to see more of the world. Under the protective umbrella of the Antioch Christian Academy and a completely supervised, non-coed roommate situation, the protective Ponticellis heartily agreed that their beautiful oldest daughter should see the world, particularly the "home country" of Italy, and specifically where the rest of their large, extended family lived, in Pisa!

I decided that the whole operation should be cloaked in the utmost secrecy. I did not want to tell Owen or my parents. I would have asked Paulo Ponticelli for his daughter's hand in marriage prior to our leaving, but I did not think he could have kept the secret for five long weeks! I had selected an engagement ring from a jeweler in Orange County and, as my father was all-knowing about my financial situation (he not only wrote my paycheck at the Block Insurance Agency but agreed to lend me the money for my second European excursion), it was a necessity of conscience to obtain the required ring down payment from an outside source. To that end, Malcolm Davis came to my rescue by fronting me the money using the cash his parents had sent him from Los Angeles for Spring semester textbook purchases. My innocent occasional drives back down to visit my best friend Malcolm Davis at college aroused no suspicion whatsoever. On one of those nights, I secretly drove home with Maria's engagement ring!

Then, to my wonderful surprise, Malcolm decided that my idea of a European graduation present the year before was a marvelous idea, so he asked his parents for the same, and they agreed! We were to be roommates again!!

So, I embarked on another whirlwind tour, only this time with my best friend and future fiancée! Maria loved the traveling and also relished getting to know a junior female student from the Antioch Christian Academy as her roommate, Lois Parkes. This trip now included the additional Scandinavian countries of Norway, Sweden, and Denmark. After four weeks of grueling travel, we finally arrived one morning in Paris, France. As soon as we were settled into the rooms of our hotel, I asked the bilingual concierge to make dinner reservations for Maria and me for the following evening at the new restaurant on the second level of the Eiffel Tower. A window table was highly preferred. Our entire group had completed a cursory tour of the city that first day, culminating in an evening cruise down the Seine River. It was extremely romantic and only enhanced my nervousness about the next, historic day.

The following morning, I woke up too early from an understandably fitful sleep. Malcolm stirred and woke up in turn as he heard my rustling about the room, frantically looking for a pair of traveling scissors to cut open my money belt. I had militantly worn the belt every waking moment of the trip, keeping it as close to me as possible, not only for the convenience and financial security but also because it housed a rather sizable investment of precious cargo!

Prior to this second European adventure, Malcolm had helped me sew Maria's engagement ring into a bottom corner of my traveling money belt, even to the paranoid extent of using thread that matched the color of the belt so as not to arouse any suspicion on Maria's part that the money belt had been unnaturally tampered with!

Four long weeks later, it was time for the cutting ceremony. The ring sparkled anew in the hotel-room light as it escaped from its month-long confinement and dropped into my clammy palm. Malcolm gave me one of his beaming smiles and hugged me. Maria and I had scheduled to be away from our group to tour Paris on our own for the entire day and evening, so I would not see my roommate again until I was, hopefully, officially "betrothed"!

It was a full day for Maria and me, commencing with a claustrophobic climb up 900 narrow, stone spiral stairs to the summit of the right-hand bell tower of Notre Dame. It felt personally rewarding to actually be looking *down* on the gargoyles that spiritually guarded the cathedral! Then we plunged down under the City of Lights to the Metro for a mad dash to the Louvre Museum. As we could spare only a small fraction of the time required to even partially absorb this mini-city of priceless possessions, I allocated two points of interest as "must sees": the Mona Lisa and the Venus de Milo. Mona was a bit of an anticlimax, and she did not look very pleased to see rushing-around tourists from America, namely us! Regardless, we stared right back at her in retaliation, feigning our very best art-appreciated faces.

As if to actually discourage those who insultingly tried to "wing it" with less than an exhaustive perusal of the full scope of the gallery, the Venus de Milo was strategically displayed at the complete other end of the football stadium-size museum. So, Maria and I were understandably winded from racing around, dodging gawking tourists with ample time on their hands and art lovers with unnaturally long attention spans, trying to reach the gigantic private shrine that housed the Venus de Milo. Upon our arrival, the chamber looked so spacious that it seemed a sad waste of square footage. But this was deliberate, artful extravagance in order to create a singular focus on the famous statue that was posed on the dais in the dead center of the room.

Maria was not up on her Greek history; her ambivalence was probably due to the fact that she was "up to here" with all things to do with the "old country" and its European neighbors. This was prompted in great measure by the incessant reminiscences of her family that could crop up at any time no matter how distant or unrelated the conversational subject was at the time.

So she couldn't have cared less about the Grecian sculpting endeavors of 2,000 years ago. She had made the frantic trek based solely on my promise to her to trust me. I told her that she would one day be very glad she would be able to say, yes, she had seen this most famous of statues. One day, she could even proudly tell her children and grandchildren.

Even so, no one had bothered to tell her that it was broken!

Maria, of course, after all of the exhausting effort spent on getting there, took one out-of-breath look at the world-renowned, revered artifact standing center stage on the expansive marble floor and at the crowds that were hopelessly transfixed on this classical achievement, seemingly oblivious to the obvious, and loudly announced,

"It's got no arms!"

Those in the room who could understand her English pronouncement as it echoed through the hall shot Maria a look of outrage and disgust. She held her own, however, with a return stare and posture of disappointment and dismay. She folded her arms and shook her head in disapproval at all of these artsy groupies who could not spot "damaged goods" when it was posing right before their very eyes!

At first, I wished that *I* was now a statue, standing off in a toga in some remote corner outside of the room! But then I realized what an invitation this event was to the new life we were going to enjoy together, this exhibition of unintimidated, hilarious honesty at its best. Grandpa Colby would have been proud of Maria. When in Paris, he might have even yelled in addition,

"And she's topless, too!"

Table number seventeen at the newly opened "La Belle Français" restaurant on the second level of the Eiffel Tower commanded a spectacular view of the rectangular fountains as they narrowed in perspective up to Trocadero Square. The sky had grown darker, and the lights had just illuminated the dancing waters as our sumptuous dinner was served. Even after a full day of Paris conquering and criticizing amputees, Maria looked spent but beautiful. After dessert, she absently turned toward the windows and stared contentedly at the brilliant water show with her chin gently resting on her hands. I seized the opportunity to quietly slide the ring box in front of her. She had noticed my movement out of the corner of her eye and looked down. "What's this?" she asked in a kind of suspicious surprise.

"Open it," I said, nervously.

The glint of the gold and the sparkle of the diamonds winked at Maria from the pinching felt of the opened ring box. She looked up at me, her eyes welling up with tears of what I hoped were dream-come-true joy. She looked down again at the never-ending circle of precious metal as I choked out the line that I had rehearsed in my head for the past six months,

"Maria, if you're not doing anything next January or February, how would you like to change your last name?"

The wedding of Ian Block to Maria Ponticelli was a grand occasion by any stretch of the imagination. We had been childhood friends, with long-standing parents in the community. We had grown up right here in the church. And then the now-famous Eiffel Tower proposal. It had "romantic fairy tale" written all over it.

Our Father's Evangelical Church Worship Center was bedecked in numerous, brilliantly colored and equally fragrant floral displays. The sloping white angel-cloth ribbons ceremoniously framed the all-important center aisle, and what appeared to be hundreds of candelabras flickered in celebration of the pending pronouncement.

The pronouncement, however, would be more stunning than intended. After we would take communion, recite our original vows to each other, and I would gingerly lift Maria's delicate veil and gave her a great big kiss, Pastor Nelson Finch would turn us both around to face the packed house and proudly exclaim, "It is my pleasure to introduce to you, for the very first time, Mr. and Mrs. *Owen* Block!" Even with the audience gasping and giggling, Pastor Finch did not detect his error until I had turned to him and gave a searching look that begged for him to retract his statement and quickly correct the matter! He had known our entire family ever since he had first arrived at Our Father's Evangelical Church and had inadvertently amalgamated all of the Block cast of characters into one big amorphous grab bag, from which he had conveniently pulled out a random name. "Well, at least I kept it in the family!" he would joke later. Little did he realize that, by virtue of our highly distinctive personalities, so much continental drift had taken place between Owen and myself over the years that his first pronouncement that day was oceans apart from the correct one.

"Excuse me, folks!" he would stammer with embarrassment. "It is my privilege to introduce to you, for the very, very first time, Mr. and Mrs. *Ian* Block!" The room would explode with relieved applause—in part for the affirmation of the new bride and groom and also in congratulations to Pastor Finch for finally figuring out who he had just married!

In the meantime, there I stood next to (more like leaning—from the tingling warnings of a swooning faint—on the everlasting arms of) Malcolm Davis, my best man, who was standing next to my brother Owen as we watched the processional of bridesmaids come down the aisle. At the very last came Angela, Maria's younger sister and also Maid of Honor. The crowd then stood in unison as the pipe organ announced "Here Comes the Bride." Slowly, arm in arm with her proud father, came the soon-to-be Maria Block. She was still breathtaking even though we had already "gone underground" to see each other prior to this encounter. As they came closer to me and the two lines of smiling groomsmen and bridesmaids, I wished that my grandparents could have been here to see this precious girl. As the organ continued with its familiar tune, and before Paulo gave up his oldest daughter's hand in marriage, I had a chance to visually soak in all of the many family and friends who had so excitedly come to see this union. I was at once flattered and amazed as I gazed out, thinking to myself, "Look at all the people!"

Upon returning from our honeymoon, we secured a small apartment in nearby Burbank and commuted to Monument for our church and job responsibilities.

Once again, we dove right into all kinds of ministry opportunities at the church. Maria and I started a "Young and Married" class over in the Educational Christianity building. Maria also sang in the church choir, as well as in a small group known as "Praiseworthy." I even went so far as to write and direct a couple of the church's Christmas programs. Not only did this busyness help me hold at bay my still-lingering holiday "loved-one loss" memories, but it also gave me the opportunity to "use my first degree" in helping wet-behind-the-ears orators grasp what was *really* foundational in any performance. Before we even auditioned any aspirants, memorized even one line, blocked any scenes, or sang any notes, I made it abundantly clear to all who were involved in the production that the absolute criterion of each heart would be to exemplify a humble "Thou shalt love the Lord thy God" perspective, lest anyone fall prey, like their Director, to the Heavenly Father's gift-exchange program!

My Christmas plays were not exactly Shakespeare, profoundly depicting the "rub" (*Hamlet*) of some Christian theological issue. They were probably more in the category of "mere prattle, without practice" (*Othello*). Regardless, they were a grass-roots effort at genuinely glorifying the Son on His birthday.

After a few years, thanks to the abundant provision of Block Insurance, we were able to purchase a beautiful home back in Monument at the end of the cul-de-sac on Chestnut Street, about a mile east of the small business building where Block Insurance resided.

Maria and I were very happy with our married life, our new home, our ministries, and our ability to spontaneously travel. It was not until three years into our matrimonial bliss that Mary walked up to Joseph after her visit to the doctor and told him to get the donkey ready!

Nine months later, after an agonizing 24-hour labor for Maria, our blessed first daughter, Sharayah, was born. Our little family was growing! We transformed one of the bedrooms in our home into a beautiful nursery, and the two of us soaked in the rapidly fleeting moments of life with a newborn. We were basking in gratitude and joy for the life God had so graciously handed to all three of us.

Like the assassination of President Kennedy, or the moonwalk of Neil Armstrong, I can remember *exactly* where I was when I received the phone call.

It was early evening on a Tuesday night in late March of 1987. Maria was in the kitchen, and I was lying on the couch, numbly watching "Jeopardy" with Sharayah sound asleep on my chest. I heard the phone ring, which fortunately did not startle or wake our new baby girl. At this age, she could remain sound asleep on the deck of an aircraft carrier during the heat of battle.

After a low-voiced preliminary conversation, Maria handed the phone to me with a look of simultaneous shock and concern on her face. On the other end of the line was a subdued Jean Worrell, not at all her usual jubilant self. She had called to relay the sad news that Sid Barrington was dead.

Sid had died of a heart attack (ironically suffering the same fate as our city's famous sculptor, Max Stellar, whose name Sid would drop frequently!) that afternoon, and the closed-casket funeral would be the upcoming Friday—one of the longest, hardest days of my life.

Due to the anticipated large crowd, the funeral was held at Forest Lawn in the Hollywood Hills. Along with the two assistants from the mortuary, it had been requested by the wife of the deceased that the original Four Musketeers be four of the six pallbearers required to haul the pachydermatous cargo from the hearse to the graveside because, as she put it, "You four were all he ever talked about, even years after he retired!"

So Nathan Raab, Kenneth Ball, Patrick Hamilton, and I came from four different parts of the country to help hoist the expired Sid Barrington from the hold of the black-curtained hearse to the hole in the brown earth at the top of the hill. I had not seen any of the other Musketeers in years. They seemed so much older now—their faces accurately recording the travails and triumphs their individual lives had dealt them. Nate was in front with me. From the other side of the casket, he looked much taller than I remember, although I am sure he thought the same about me, the "bean sprout!" His blond hair was thinning on top, and he seemed quite preoccupied with this whole affair. We were all reeling in our own way, recalling in relentless waves memory after memory forever attached to our childhood mentor now in the pine box.

The six of us laid the casket next to the rectangular opening that interrupted the spacious lawns and took our places among the crowd. I stood next to Owen (who was strangely silent and stern, perhaps from guilt as he had not been doing much "church goin'" these days), and my mom and dad. Seated next to us in specially designated chairs were the very elderly Mrs. Mackintosh and Mrs. Hawkins.

Our Father's Evangelical Church's new pastor, Sheldon Abbott, delivered a mechanical eulogy. It was not entirely his fault, as our church was his first senior pastorate and this his first solo funeral. He had met Sid only once, in the hospital, a few weeks earlier, when Sid's heart had given his body a warning signal.

So, Pastor Abbott walked us through the expected green pastures and still waters of Psalm 23 in a novice, lackluster attempt to restore our souls. But my wandering mind was page-turning through a thick mental photo album replete with the impact that this 5th- and 6th-grade Sunday school teacher had permanently had upon my life. We all sang the standard "Amazing Grace" as Sid's body was lowered into its final resting place. In flashes, I was remembering countless Sunday school classes, special outdoor lessons in the park, or just hanging out at the childless Barrington house, eating Esmeralda's to-die-for lasagna. What a foundation this pillar had poured for the four of us. The life's survival kit that he, in part, had handed down to us was now being utilized to come to grips with his own passing.

"... *Through many dangers, toils, and snares I have already come. 'Tis grace that brought me safe thus far, and grace will lead me home ...*"

I wanted so badly to talk with Sid just once more! I had not seen him for quite some time. The only carrot dangling in front of me was found in our continued hopeful singing,

"*When we've been there ten thousand years, bright shining as the sun. We've no less days to sing God's praise than when we first begun ...*"

I asked God to forgive me for thinking that singing His eternal praises was not nearly as important just now as that moment of being able to stand next to Synopsis Sid again.

We then sang Sid's favorite hymn, "I Sing the Mighty Power of God." Nathan Raab had come alongside me. "Can you believe it, Ian? I can't believe he's gone!"

"*. . . While all that borrows life from Thee is ever in Thy care . . .*"

"Neither can I," I choked out. The hillside was mobbed with mourners, all dressed in the traditional black. They looked like a bunch of ravens in an odd reversal of biblical fortunes, as *they* were the ones who had been miraculously fed by the Elijah in the coffin. The service closed with choir member Bonnie Metcalf singing what we all were feeling so deeply,

I dreamed I went to Heaven and you were there with me,
we walked upon the streets of gold beside the crystal sea.
We heard the angels singing
then someone called your name,
You turned and saw this young man
and he was smiling as he came.
And he said, "Friend, you may not know me now"
And then he said, "But wait,
you used to teach my Sunday school
When I was only eight.

And every week you would say a prayer
before class would start,

and one day when you said that prayer
I asked Jesus in my heart.

Thank you for giving to the Lord
for I am a life that was changed.
Thank you for giving to the Lord,
I'm so glad you gave."

One by one they came as far as the eye could see,
each life somehow touched by your generosity.
Little things that you had done,
Sacrifices made,
unnoticed on the Earth,
In Heaven now proclaimed,

And I know up in Heaven, you're not supposed to cry,
But I'm almost sure,
there were tears in your eyes,
as Jesus took your hand,
and you stood before the Lord. He said,
'My child, look around you,
For great is your reward!'

As they say, "There wasn't a dry eye in the place!" After
the service, the majority of the crowd lingered in individual,
pensive tribute.

Esmeralda came up to me. In spite of her loss and grief after
nearly 50 years of marriage to Sid, she looked marvelous in a
spanking new, crisp black dress complete with elegant veil. She
hugged me and whispered "You know, Ian, Sid just *adored* you.
He saw so much potential in you." I could not stop the tears

from coming and stood there shaking in her arms. She eventually let go of the embrace, as if desirous to change the subject, and stared out over the hillside at the sea of people, beneficiaries of all ages unable to stop paying their respects to their beloved fallen saint. Esmeralda herself even seemed surprised at the massive attendance, testimony to the vast impact her husband had had in that 10 x 12 Sunday school room and beyond.

She shook her head in amazement as she put her arm around me and half said to herself,

"Look at all the people!"

PART TWO

CHAPTER FIVE

THIS IS THE PARSON . . .

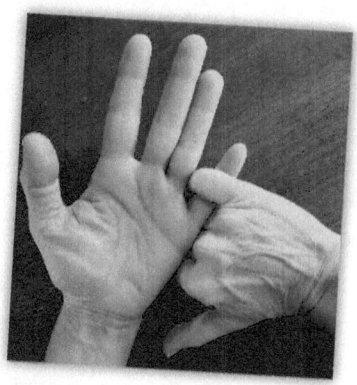

"And, so, my brothers and sisters, it is with a heavy heart that I have tendered my resignation to your Deacon Board effective immediately. I, I do so deeply apologize, even though I know it does not seem enough, I just want, I want you to know how remorseful I feel having so blatantly betrayed you, my beloved flock, after all these years . . . I am heartbroken at the grief this has caused my family, Jenny, Jordan and Elliot . . . I can only hope and pray that I can begin the task of repairing . . ."

I was sitting in the front row of the Worship Center of Our Father's Evangelical Church, deacon-dressed to the hilt on that eventful Sunday morning. My legs were crossed, and my head was down; my eyes were closed, with my thumb and index finger pinching the bridge of my nose. I could not bear to watch him speak.

It was so pitiful. I was so embarrassed for him.

It was so very, very sad.

Before the Chairman of the Deacon Board, Samuel Caldwell, came to the pulpit to try to find the bottom that had dropped out from under the congregation, it was unanimously agreed by the Deacon Board that Senior Pastor Sheldon Abbott should first personally confess his adulterous relationship with Tatiana Kincaid to the entire flock.

I had found out during a specially called Deacon Board meeting the previous week. I knew something was amiss just by the sound of the usually boisterous Chairman of the Board's now-tremulous voice over the phone. The air was thick when I walked into the special deacon meeting, held in one of the Educational Christianity Sunday school rooms. It was a prophetic cloud the size of a man's hand that bespoke the torrent of unwanted rain that was about to fall on the corner of Valentino and Ridgeway Avenues.

The faces of the other members of the Deacon Board were morose. They had been tipped off by various means of communication prior to the official meeting as to what was going down. Pastor Abbott looked stricken. His face was as white as a sheet, and he was looking down at the forest-green carpet of the Sunday school room.

"Hello, Ian," said Samuel Caldwell, in a measured tone that tried to portray personable congeniality and official sobriety all at once. "Please, have a seat, son."

"Thanks," I returned. I found an empty chair at the long rectangular table. The eyes of the other members of the board watched me sit down; Pastor Abbott's eyes never broke their fixation with the carpet. Since he had been far more joyous and outgoing with me upon first sight at all of our previous board meetings, it did not take much Solomonic wisdom to ascertain that the gloomy, as-yet-undisclosed subject matter silently hovering over the room had his name written all over it.

After some opening remarks by Chairman Caldwell, in the categories of apology for the spontaneity of the meeting called, and appreciation for our unanimous attendance on the occasion, he gave "the floor" to Pastor Abbott, who already seemed to be quite riveted to it.

Pastor Abbott looked up and slowly launched into a laborious confession. He began with his now-disclosed long-term problem of being attracted to older women, stemming from his promiscuous youth all the way up to his current magnet, Tatiana Kincaid. The affair had exploded to smithereens when enough evidence reached his wife, Jenny Abbott, to forcefully confront her lately preoccupied, frequently-absent-at-Pastors Conferences husband, which led to the first of what were to be many painful confessions.

All eyes seemed to be fixated upon me, the 36-year-old youngest member of the Deacon Board, to see how I was taking this shocking news.

For some unknown reason, my first reaction was a mental one. I made a quick and complete assessment of those privileged souls who had departed Earth prior to this horrific moment and were thus to be spared from the ecclesiastical holocaust that was to come. It had been 10 years since Sid Barrington's funeral. Henceforth, Our Father's Evangelical Church had lost Doris Mackintosh, Cyril Holbert (Deacon Holbert's charter-member father), Bonnie Metcalf, Mrs. Hawkins, and even that prune Virgil Cronklin was not going to have to endure the future conflagration heating up on the other side of the church's front door—just to name a few.

The end result of this mental parade of the dearly departed was my feeling of aloneness—a disconnection from my past—and a complete inadequacy as to what the appropriate reaction should be on my part. When Pastor Abbott was finished with his sordid retrospective, I was as white as he was.

I did not know Tatiana Kincaid that well, although speculations on the exact level of her inherited wealth abounded in the gossip and rumor chambers among the rank-and-file of the church. I had the distinct impression that she did not like me very much. This might be my misinterpretation of the aloofness she exuded from some socioeconomic barrier she apparently embraced. There was, however, much conjecture at the Deacon Board level as to whether those large, anonymous chunks of money occasionally received by the church were in fact Tatiana's tithing from her magnificent opulence. After tonight, I suspected they were sin offerings given in compensation for her meretricious behavior with the Senior Pastor right underneath our ignorant noses.

But Pastor Abbott was another matter altogether. "How could you?" I blurted out when he had put his head back down in order to re-establish his staring contest with the carpet. "How could you, Pastor Abbott?" I had fully trusted him. I had gone to him for counseling issues. He had dedicated both of our daughters. My anger began to boil, and my communication began to lose its discretion. "I am only glad you were not here to marry Maria and me. Thank God Pastor Finch had that privilege. Think how tainted I would feel just now about my own marriage, when I think of you standing there, officiating, all the while harboring this sexual penchant for attractive, rich, older women!" I stood up from the table.

Two spirits suddenly collided with my own in giving me contradictory advice from their own past examples. My "walk out and never look back" deacon grandfather engaged in a responsibility tug-o-war with my "stick it out to the bitter end" deacon father.

"How could you?" I said again from my standing position while looking down at the deflated Pastor Abbott. He slowly raised his head to me, a hang-dog look in his reddened eyes.

"I am so sorry, Ian. As I have thought about this meeting, I worried about your reaction to this most of all, and what you would think of me. I hope you will someday find it in your heart to forgive me."

"Forgive you?"

I was seething.

I stepped back from my chair, positioning myself for the door, obsequiously mimicking the *Colby* Block method of making a point, while my father's example simultaneously shook its head in grave disappointment.

"Please sit down, Ian." It was Chairman Caldwell. His authoritative and beseeching gaze bored into my soul like the spiritual referee that I so desperately needed. "Please, Ian, have a seat, and we can discuss this further."

"How can you possibly ask me to forgive you, Pastor Abbott?" I said, blatantly ignoring the Chairman's ameliorating invitation, "after what you have just done?"

"Ian, please!" implored Chairman Caldwell.

My knocking knees abruptly flexed their bodily authority and made the decision for my soul and spirit that would affect me for the rest of my life.

I sat back down.

The Sunday morning service ended with Chairman Caldwell outlining the church's procedure for: The intensified account-ability of the current Senior Pastor, the foraging for forgiveness

THIS IS THE CHURCH...

for the current Senior Pastor, the rapid expulsion of the current Senior Pastor, and the immediate replacement search party to be formed for a new Senior Pastor, all the while trying to lovingly embrace the dispossessed immediate family of the current Senior Pastor.

His methodical speech struck me as a bit too pragmatic for the shocked and devastated congregation. His strategy was, no doubt, to assure the jaded church members that the salacious situation would be handled circumspectly and with calm. "Order" was the order of the day, and the Deacon Board would see to it that the flock's perception of their elected leadership would instill confidence in the "system" that they would meticulously oversee. In a word: Chairman Caldwell was determined to hold down the fort with not so much as a gasp of hysteria.

In spite of Chairman Caldwell not fully addressing the obvious breadth of emotions—surprise, disappointment, anger, rage, and all the rest—that had rolled over the congregation as each new development was divulged during Sheldon Abbott's scandalous confessional, he, in hindsight, had a wise hand on the pulse rate of the church and set a rock-solid example for the other members of the board, as stormy weather was on the horizon.

"Gentlemen, at all costs, keep your nose to the grindstone. Tread carefully with the procedures. Do not be distracted by the groundswell of mayhem that might ensue from any quarter of the congregation. If we are going to have a church left after the dust has settled on the Abbott affair, we are going to have to hold it together with a tenacity that might seem insensitive to some within our membership. Do not give an ear to the ambulance chasers—let them run after their own sirens. You will have enough wreckage here to deal with. We must show a united front with a realistic plan for preserving the wall as soon as the word gets out that Humpty Dumpty has fallen!"

Even with the pejorative slip of the nursery-rhyme illusion of the Senior Pastor, it was an inspired charge given to the Board on that night when I had first heard the news (after we had dismissed Sheldon Abbott from the Sunday school room). Chairman Caldwell did not realize how inspired he was in articulating our marching orders with such perspicacity, as it would truly become the glue that would sustain us during the land mines, crossfires, and "take no prisoners" season Our Father's Evangelical Church was embarking upon.

Understandably, the congregation that Sunday morning had as many varied reactions as there were members present. The "united front" Deacon Board was ready for action! We were sporadically seated throughout the Worship Center so as to be accessible and approachable after the service and field any questions or just be a sounding board. Pastor Abbott had quickly been exited off the stage (without the necessity of a shepherd's crook) and just as quickly ushered out the back of the sanctuary after his little "chat" with his flock.

Sam and Betsy Morley came up to me immediately after the closing song (it had narrowly finished), as they were seated right behind me. They had greeted me prior to the service with their usual gusto and enthusiasm. Their joy in the Lord was sometimes baffling as they had blended two families into one with their marriage six years ago. Both prior on-the-rocks marriages had produced three children. By the time Sam and Betsy tied the knot, the six combined children were well along in age. Since the prior spouses wanted some semblance of a relationship with their natural offspring, multiple plate-spinning commenced as soon as the Morleys returned from their Hawaiian honeymoon. Their daily lives were a chaotic blend of bread-winning, taxi-driving, and awkward role-playing—all indicative of the jockeying-for-custody settlements agreed upon as the outcome of their rather bitter previous divorces.

Their wedding had been packed with a standing-room-only crowd at Our Father's Evangelical Church. It would be called "the Wedding of the Century"—not only for its interesting "Brady Bunch" mathematics, but also because the audience that Saturday afternoon in June was primarily filled with the self-appointed "Cupids" of the church who, by hook, crook, or arrow, had been determined to bring these two together.

The Morleys kept a sense of humor throughout the whole meddlesome courtship. Betsy even agreed to forgo the standard wedding statues on the top of their wedding cake. Instead, they placed two figurines who were sitting in chairs *flat on their backs* on the top tier of the cake. The surface was frosted to look exactly like the restaurant floor on that momentous night when Sam had made his first move on Betsy.

They were not nearly as joyful at the end of the service as they were during our greeting at the outset. Sam's face was red with hornet's nest fury as he approached me. He was so angry he even put his face far into that psychological "space" one maintains around one's own. I tried to courteously step back, but he kept regaining ground with each new hostile sentence.

"Ian, did you know about this?" he snorted truculently.

"I, I found out last Tuesday." I quivered, knowing that in Sam's present volcanic mood, any prior knowledge of these circumstances before they were divulged to the church at large would be perceived not as thoughtful leadership but as an underhanded hiding of the facts.

I let him continue erupting. "Do you know that he counseled us?"

He nodded toward Betsy, who was standing beside him with a faraway look in her eyes. She had the presence of mind to nod in agreement with whatever it was that Sam was saying. Sam had not taken his eyes off of mine.

"I can't believe he actually sat there in his office, in his big leather burgundy chair, and had the audacity to give us advice on 'blended families'! He had pictures of Jenny and the kids all over his desk—what a family man, huh? What a—"

"Sam!" Betsy jumped in, afraid that her trenchant Sam would regret the colorful adjective he had chosen in the heat of the moment that was ready to take an irretrievable swan dive off his tongue. Betsy knew her husband well enough to run interference when needed (like Carmel's crazy couple, Abigail and Nabal, contriving their way through 1st Samuel, Chapter 25) and protect not only Sam's modest reputation of decorum, but my novice deacon impressions as well.

I cut in before things became too uncomfortable: "We are doing everything we can to—"

"To what?" Sam interrupted.

His retort was not giving me much conversational space, which I perceived to be an insult to my Deacon Board youthfulness as well as my obvious inexperience in all things pastoral-immoral. "Well," I stammered, "you know, to, to get things straightened out."

"How can you straighten out a low-life, practicing adulterer?"

"Sam! We need to go!" Betsy was courteous, but forceful, and Sam knew the jig was up. He said nothing more as Betsy grabbed his arm and turned him to leave.

"I am so sorry, Ian, I'll be . . . *we'll* be praying for you!" These were her parting words as she stopped the circulation in Sam's forearm and ushered her red-faced husband out of the building before he could exacerbate the situation any further.

I turned to leave myself, to quickly find Maria and snatch up Sharayah and Samantha from the "Come Unto Me" Children's Church program and get home as rapidly as possible. Chairman Caldwell saw me out of the corner of his eye and cut short his conversation with Troy Cobb, the church organist, in order to approach me. "Excuse me, Troy," I heard him say. "I will talk to you soon, okay?" With this abrupt closure, he was able to turn and flag me down. "Ian! A minute, please!"

"Yes, sir?"

"Ian, we are meeting again this Tuesday to select church members for a Pastoral Search Committee. Can we count on you to attend?"

"Uh, okay . . . sure." I conveyed far more enthusiasm than I honestly felt. I had already endured one special meeting last Tuesday over and above our regular monthly vigils to hear our blubbering, defrocked Senior Pastor introduce the skeletons in his closet, which was capped off with this morning's highly charged "tell all" bombshell. The last thing I wanted to do was to leave my young family *again* and head to the church for another special deacon meeting!

"Are you sure, Ian? It is very important that we get things underway. Troy Cobb has agreed to ask his father to pinch-hit for us in the pulpit for a spell. His father is a retired pastor, and he lives close by. But I do not want to take too much advantage of his willingness, and I also do not want to risk him overstaying his welcome. The church can handle a temporary fix for only so long before it starts to unravel. So, we need to show them we are on the move, right?"

"Right!" *I'd rather be on a beach in Maui, reading a book.*

"Great! We'll see you this Tuesday!" I had the distinct impression that the robust, white-haired, sixty-something Chairman Caldwell would *not* rather be on a beach in Maui. Truth be told, I think he actually *enjoyed* this kind of challenge. He most certainly had the brass and bandwidth for it. He had already been on a beach once, as a part of the Normandy invasion during World War II, so I think our little dilemma here at O.F.E. let him reminisce a bit.

I called my father that afternoon when our Sunday lunch was finished. I needed the reassurance I knew he could provide. "Ian, believe me, this, too, shall pass," he had said in response to my doom-and-gloom ranting and raving into the receiver. He had not served on the Deacon Board for quite a while, but he had amassed enough wisdom over the years he had served on the board to give his discouraged son a verbal postcard of the big picture.

He and my mother were still very active at the church—ushering, serving communion, teaching, hosting socials and Bible studies at their home. He had just felt that it was high time for new blood on the board, so he wanted to make room. It was not long before "Uncle Sam" called up my number and conscripted me to serve, which I did willingly. Six months later, the special meeting was called, and Our Father's Evangelical Church was thrown into a nasty season of transition. New blood is one thing—*bloodshed* is quite another!

"You're going to have to forgive him, you know." It was Maria. I had just closed my eyes after lying down on our bed for my coveted Sunday-afternoon nap. She had checked on our girls and come right into our bedroom. Her statement of fact was announced before she had even shut the door behind her. "Who?" I asked, opening my eyes and turning to look at her. I knew exactly who; I just wanted to hear her say it and give me a darn good reason why!

"You know who, Ian! Pastor Abbott! You need to forgive him."

"Maybe, maybe not!" I said poutingly, my eyes closed again.

"Ian, look at me!"

I obeyed.

"You will not be able to lead this church wisely unless you are purposefully in the process of forgiving Sheldon Abbott."

"It's far too soon!" I said curtly.

"At least give God your heart in the matter," she responded. It seemed to me a pat statement, but, coming from Maria, I knew it was her way of describing my only hope as she sincerely saw it.

"God can only have the pieces because that is all that's left!" My lower lip hung down for dramatic emphasis. Maria saw right through my facial special effects.

"That's exactly what God thrives on!" And she left the room.

Forgive Sheldon Abbott? With what? I was in no condition to turn the other cheek and do that *seventy times seven* routine. But was that even a prerequisite? Frankly, I just did not *want* to forgive him right now! I kind of *enjoyed* being mad at him, wallowing around in betrayed self-pity. Maria could at least grant me that, couldn't she? After all, I'm just not in the right frame of mind to—

"That's exactly what God thrives on!" Sometimes I hate it when Maria is right.

The moment I even contemplated the idea of forgiveness, other foreign emotions flooded in, convoluting my festering wrath. I began to actually feel some compassion for the plight of this man and the awful, lifelong repercussions his dalliances would bring upon his family. *How could you, Pastor Abbott? How could you throw in the foot-washing towel for trollop Tatiana*

Kincaid's inherited thirty pieces of silver? How could you? And your sons Jordan and Elliot. What have you done to them? I wouldn't get too close to any ample bodies of water if I were you, as you have two millstones the size of Texas around your neck!

Admittedly, it was a long way from forgiveness. But was my cheek at least turning ever so slightly?

Our phone rang off the hook. Companion phones were doing the same in all the other board members' houses. The people at Our Father's Evangelical Church were experiencing the predicted gamut of emotional responses and were venting to the board at every opportunity. Like the sunburn of Moses, the board unanimously acquired the same complexion—only ours was not from divine dictation at high altitudes. Ours was from sounding-board windburn as we were blown and buffeted by many different velocities of hot and cold opinionated air.

Jenny Abbott was not seen again at the church. A few of her closest friends tried to hang onto their friendship with her and keep the fragile communication lines open. The church genuinely tried their best to love her, but there was no one to hug. She went to live with her older brother out of state and took sons Jordan and Elliot with her. The church chased her with cards and letters lovingly imploring her to come back home and let the Body help her heal. She would have none of it. Her response was to slap her estranged husband with divorce papers demanding full custody of their two sons. I am sure her emotions had just snapped after the news was finally broken and she assessed the matrimonial damage. Yet her discarding of those relationships that sought to come alongside her only caused a cloud of suspicion to form over her reactionary behavior and dared even those closest to her to suspect that age-old adage, "You know, it takes *two* . . . " Or, one!

Likewise, Our Father's Evangelical Church did everything possible to win back brother Abbott and drive him through the accountability car wash. He went along with the process initially with a contrived graciousness. Under the board's oversight, Sheldon Abbott did a pretty convincing job in the repentance department for his skulduggery. But he soon was contorting himself under our collective grip and finally broke away from any hope of restoration. With certain undaunted members of the Deacon Board still trying to hold on for dear life, Sheldon Abbott moved away—taking new wife Tatiana Kincaid with him. He was likely to be reinstated as a Senior Pastor somewhere by a church that would provide the appropriate cover under a unique witness-protection program that hid wayward leaders in rock clefts not wanting to come face to face with how they got there.

I had turned to my tried-and-true method of teaching, the synopsis, as my indignation coping mechanism. One Sunday shortly after "The Great Confession," I gave the "Young and Married" class a synopsis on the most famous adulterous affair in all of the Bible, with no clever gimmicks this time.

"*Palace Place* has been number one in the television ratings for years. This is primarily due to its tawdry, soap-opera story line and ridiculous premise. It pits a king against all odds to see if he can survive the most sensational of challenges. One episode, 'Family Feud,' featured the king as the only son remaining after each of his brothers are rudely disqualified from the show. Another episode was loaded with special effects and gore as the king is seen sawing off the head of a very tall rival contestant. The episode 'Roofwatch' received particularly high ratings as it featured this king with a beautiful extra from the

'Gladiators Illustrated No-Toga 990 B.C. Calendar' issue. It was a two-part drama which included mayhem, murder, battles, and betrayals. Some of the sponsors received complaints from the viewers who said that the show was full of too much sex and violence. Their response was to cancel the show outright and replace it with a children's program called *Mr. Nathan's Neighborhood*. In the show, the host tells silly fables involving rich and poor men's sheep. The king from the *Palace Place* show could no longer find work and asked if he could play the part of the rich man in one of Mr. Nathan's stories. Mr. Nathan said that would be 'type-casting'!"

"Please open your Bibles to 1st Samuel."

I then launched into a "Taking God Seriously" lesson that did not paint a pretty picture of the "man after God's own heart" or of the man after Tatiana's.

"The child died!" I had pronounced with finality to the class, referring to David and Bathsheba's "oops."

"In the Middle East somewhere, there is a gravestone that reads 'Tomb of the Unknown Child'—a rather disturbing 'Ebenezer' to all those who think it's easier to ask God for forgiveness than it is for permission!"

I could feel the passion boiling up in my teaching from the realization that a little bit of Ian had recently died, too. Only these children were not nameless. They were called "Trust" and "Admiration" and were buried under hard-packed gravel with disreputable Sheldon Abbott's piratical "X" marking the spot.

Newly-out-of-mothballs retired "Reverend" (that's what he liked to be called) Cobb did a fair job at filling the recklessly abandoned pulpit. He tried to biblically encourage us to not worry by "raven watching" and "lily pondering." He noted that, by example, ravens are naturally happy with their divinely delivered bird food, as are lilies with their royalty-rivaling wardrobes. This all was a little hard to swallow, however. As the weeks and months wore on, a good number of the "ravens" in the congregation were flying south for the winter, and many of the "lilies" were now showing up only at Easter.

As prophesied by Chairman Caldwell, without a permanent Senior Pastor, our numbers were precipitously dwindling. Our congregation eroded down to one-third its previous Sheldon Abbott-era size with all the absentees bitterly finding or founding other churches outside of Monument. These fractious transients would require a mountain of forgiveness (that could only come from the Supreme Head of the church in the first place) by the remaining, deserted remnant at Valentino and Ridgeway Avenues—including me!

The only trouble was I had *no idea* how or where to start!

And that was only the beginning.

My father had agreed to serve on the Pastoral Search Committee, along with Deacon Holbert and a cast of characters representing each flavorful slice of the O.F.E. pie.

The search went on for nearly two years! "Reverend" Cobb barely lasted a year. The Search Committee brought in three "trial and error" interim pastoral candidates who were a good dose of both. The leadership of the church could never seem to "make a deal" with the candidate behind door number one—who lasted two months—the candidate behind door number two—who lasted four months, and the candidate behind door number three—who lasted three months. The balance of Sundays were glued together with missionary speakers and traveling evangelists.

If only the Search Committee, like wayfaring teacher-priest Ezra with a dearth of Levites forming cavities in his caravan, could have sent out a Search Party to that magical land of Casiphia, where ministers of all shapes and sizes seemed to grow on trees—just ripe for the pickin'!

But on *this* side of the Jordan River, the protracted season of slim pickin's was interminable! The board was barraged with anxious questions about the status of the search. Everywhere you turned, there was some member of the congregation who sought you out for a progress report—whether at an open house of the John Adams Elementary School, picking up a video at the video store, or standing in line for a teller at the Monument Savings and Loan. I might as well have worn a white T-shirt with emblazoned black letters saying, "Ask Me About Our Pastor Void!"

Finally, candidate number four arrived! A young, tall, dark man about a year older than myself. He was fresh out of seminary up in Washington State. His name was Milton Derringer. On his first Sunday, he walked up to the pulpit in a jet-black suit, confidently grabbed both sides of the lectern, and looked out at the more-crowded-than-usual Worship Center.

"I know my name sounds like some sheriff in a Zane Grey western novel, but I assure you that the only badge I wear says, 'Child of the King,' the only weapon in my holster is the Word of God, and the only paper in my hand is a 'Wanted:' poster with a mug shot of the Devil!"

Cute. Very cute. Very rehearsed (he had obviously used this opener before). He sounded more to me like a permanent staff escapee from the Cheyenne Christian Conference Center. But it worked! The crowd was won over by this charming new candidate.

He was confirmed as "God's man" within weeks. He moved his family down to Southern California (including his wife,

Amber, and four biblically named boys: Joshua, David, Matthew, and Andrew) from Washington State. It was not long before the name on the marquee at the corner of Valentino and Ridgeway Avenues (under the catchy, weekly sermon title) read, "Pastor Milton Derringer, preaching."

His first agenda as a brand-new pastor was to get to know his new Deacon Board, and he decided to start at the bottom rung, with the youngest member. Because laypeople attempt ministries outside of their other responsibilities of making a living and family obligations, any required church meetings are pushed to the extreme ends of daylight hours. Hence, evening board meetings can meander into the wee hours of the night, and the infamous breakfast meeting at the *other* end of the nocturnal spectrum occurs in equivalent darkness, long before God wakes up and roosters barely think of crowing, even twice.

The restaurant of choice must be open 24 hours in order to accommodate this bipolar schedule of the church lay-leader. At one of these pre-dawn gatherings, I met with Pastor Derringer and Chairman Caldwell for the express purpose of my getting to know the new pastor and he me. After the official hand-shaking ceremony, I slid into the booth, strategically situated in a far corner of the restaurant. I was relieved that "Uncle Sam" was going to join us for my inaugural conversation with the guy who wears the "Child of the King" badge. But, to my horror, before the lugubrious, bleary-eyed, night-shift waitress had even taken our breakfast order, Chairman Caldwell excused himself! "Well, I'll be leaving now. So long, Pastor, Ian. Enjoy your breakfast!" With that, he grabbed his coat and was gone. The World War II hero was now a deserter! The seaplane had landed on the desert isle and had only rescued *one* passenger, leaving the other two behind, toes dug in the sand, to fend for themselves!

"So, Ian, how long have you been a Christian?" Pastor Derringer did not waste any time and did not believe in small talk. For the next three hours over pancakes, toast, and innumerable cups of coffee, Milton Derringer received an earful of Ian Block—everything from Mrs. Hawkins to Sid Barrington, from the Cheyenne Christian Conference Center to the Antioch Christian Academy. As I grew accustomed to this interrogation, I reversed the spotlight toward this man from the state of Washington who was so close to my own age. He was biblically grounded, articulate, a visionary, and *just right* for Monument's only church.

"You are going to be a great pastor," I concluded.

"And so are you!" he replied.

"Excuse me?" This career change was news to me!

"Ian, I am not going to be the only pastor at Our Father's Evangelical Church."

"You're not?" I started to panic at the possibilities!

"No." Sheriff Derringer then proceeded to spell out his intentions to deputize the entire Deacon Board into pastors. No longer would the congregation perceive only the "Senior" Pastor as the Moses of Monument who baptizes, prays, eulogizes, communes, and visits the sick.

This Moses was very seriously taking his Midianite father-in-law's advice to *delegate*.

"I can't do this on my own, Ian. The church is too large and too complicated. We all need to become operating pastors for this Body to excel. We need to change the perception of the people to see the Deacon Board in this way."

When we left the restaurant (the sun had actually risen by then), we shook hands in the parking lot, preparing to walk to our separate cars (my Ford Mustang had long since been substituted with a more conventional, family-friendly Honda Accord).

"Goodbye, *Sheriff* Derringer!" I said, giving my new friend a good-natured smile.

His return volley was also served with a smile, and was sobering:

"Goodbye, *Pastor* Block!"

The first position I played as a new "pastor" was defensive linebacker in order to "block" the offensive lines of the contentious blowhards who began tooting their horns of "foul play" the minute Pastor Derringer hit the field.

I took shots on Milton's behalf from every direction: His sermons were not deep enough, long enough, holy enough, short enough, funny enough, biblical enough, serious enough, challenging enough, realistic enough, far-fetched enough, provocative enough, applicable enough, gospel enough, personal-illustration enough, altar-call enough, gestures enough, hair-combed-right enough, suit-pressed enough, teeth-white enough—*already, enough!*

Pastor Derringer might have been better off just standing at the podium in utter silence, staring at the congregation for 45 minutes! Although he probably would have received another critical letter that his sermons were not "loud enough!"

He also took hits on the quality of his marriage, how he raised his kids, the car he drove, the size of his house and its upkeep, the restaurants he frequented, the company he kept, the music he liked. I was tackled for my pathetic blocks, and the tackles became catfights, and the catfights became dogpiles, and the dogpiles became brawls—and the Great Wonderful Counselor Prince of Peace Referee never once threw down a penalty flag!

The honeymoon was over!

The Senior Pastor had rolled over in bed the next morning and discovered his congregation without any makeup, unshaven, curlers in its hair, scratching, sniffing, belching, and . . . leaving!

And what an exodus it was! Long-time charter members and short-term window shoppers alike all moved toward the exit signs, each with their own ridiculous reasons for not wanting to call Our Father's Evangelical Church home any longer. Their manufactured walking papers cited the most trumped-up charges against our new Senior Pastor and were used as pathetic excuses for God calling them elsewhere. Both close friends and distant acquaintances made it a special point to tell *me*, the young deacon, just why they were leaving. In order to justify their intentions, they would describe for me the maverick new pastor and the moribund condition of the church as they saw it. It appeared that *I* was the one who was deceived into thinking that the church was, in fact, safely on the narrow road and not making some maniacal U-turn with Derringer at the wheel.

As our detractors were bellowing over their shoulders on the way out, I remembered what I had overheard my father say to my mother so many years before:

"They never close their mouths long enough to *listen* to the Almighty as they are too busy heaving cannonballs of accusations and tabloid rumors over the walls of the church!"

I was now in the very maelstrom my father had weathered quite a few times. I was anchored by his counsel throughout my feelings of abandonment, betrayal, bitterness, and resentment toward the fair-weather O.F.E. membership, who jumped like rats from a ship they thought was sinking. If they had had the backbone to wait out the typhoon of adjustment, they would have become a crew on a ship that was actually soaring!

How Pastor Derringer could run and not grow weary, walk and not faint during this season of growing pains was beyond me. I went into his office one day with the express purpose of having him answer my perplexities.

"It's the indisputable call of God, Ian. I am certain, beyond a shadow of a doubt, that God has called me here. If I wasn't so convinced, I would have buckled months ago. But before I sound too pious, let me show you something."

Pastor Derringer then opened a lower drawer in his desk and pulled out a Manila file folder. "You know what this is?" he said. I shook my head.

"These are all of the letters of encouragement that I have received since the first day I candidated here. When I am under fire and can't stand the heat any longer, I will look through these letters, and they help me get through."

I nodded, wondering if the couple of notes I had sent him had made it into the file. Satisfied, I stood to leave. Before I reached his office door, Pastor Derringer also stood up from his desk and called to me, "Oh, Ian!"

"Yeah." I stopped and turned around back toward the office interior.

"One more thing," the Pastor said as he came up to me in the office doorway and put his arm around me. "From one pastor to another—even with an assurance of the call of God, and a file of nice, affirming letters, I would not be still standing here having subjected myself and family to the most vicious judgment and backbiting ever levied against us, without one more thing."

"What's that?" I asked, my curiosity piqued.

He smiled, "Forgiveness."

Maria caught me one evening later that week in our spare-bedroom-turned-office, writing at my desk in the corner.

"What are you doing, Honey?"

I had quickly spun around in the desk chair in an obvious gesture of wanting to keep my endeavors under a cloak of secrecy.

Undeterred, Maria brazenly walked right up to the desk and looked over my shoulder to the paper that was concealed under my hands and arms.

"What are you writing? A letter?" she persisted.

"Yes," I confessed.

"To whom?"

"Oh, it's nothing. I was just writing something."

"To whom?"

"It's just a letter I am trying to write to someone. It's a catharsis thing; I have no intention of actually mailing it, so—"

"To *whom*, Ian!"

I sighed. "Sheldon Abbott."

CHAPTER SIX

Going Upstairs . . .

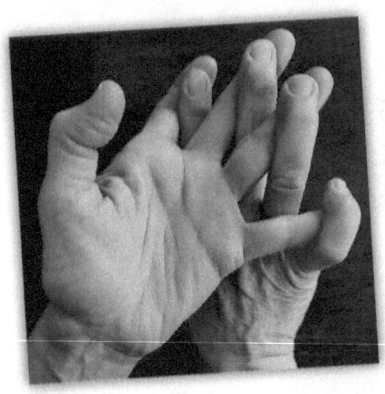

". . . and they lived happily ever after."

I gently closed the large tome that was full of the fantastic feats and foibles of princes and princesses, dwarves and ogres, castles and curses, good over evil, and leaned over to kiss Samantha's forehead.

After she had said her enviable prayers of such natural child-like simplicity and honesty, and I had performed the obligatory "This is the church, this is the steeple . . ." by popular demand, I kissed her again and said softly into her ear,

"Good night, Sweetheart."

"Goodnight, Daddy! I love you!"

"I love you, too. Sleep well."

With that, Samantha rolled over in her comforter toward the wall and was soon fast asleep. I took advantage of that parental moment to savor all of this. I looked around her seven-year-old room; the Winnie-the-Pooh wallpaper, the horse posters, the little white desk and chest of drawers, the shelves crammed with stuffed animals. After completing my scan of Samantha's room for future memories' sake, my eyes returned to the sleeping mound in the bed, and I visually "dusted" for those "fingerprints of God."

"Thanks, Lord," I muttered to myself in satisfied conclusion at Samantha safely sleeping in her cozy bed in her adorable room on the second story of our delightful home on Chestnut Street— the embodiment of that "middle station" in life as described by Robinson Crusoe's father. We are truly blessed! I closed the door—only partway—behind me (by her explicit orders—she, like her parents, was only too human and harbored occasional dark fears that could be eliminated only by the penetrating light from the hallway)—and ventured back down the stairs with the large book of fairy tales still weighing heavily under my arm.

This particular season of a father's life must be one of the best. Especially that time in the evening when we go upstairs after dinner and play time, homework and chores, baths and teeth brushing, when I can lie down with my daughters in their beds and introduce them to the population found in the wonderful world of books.

My attraction to, fascination with, and affection for the literary world was truly ignited once upon a specific time. In 3rd grade, our class took an introductory trip to the school library. We were free to choose any book that struck our fancy and read quietly for the next 45 minutes. I randomly picked up Kenneth Graham's *The Wind in the Willows,* primarily because of Ernest H. Shepard's hilarious illustrations, and the fact that it was on a shelf at eye-level with my height. Reading through the book, especially the rollicking exploits of motorcar-stealing Toad and his scrapes with the police, it suddenly dawned on me that what I was holding in my hands was actually the original source material for Disneyland's "Mr. Toad's Wild Ride!" The pages I was turning suddenly became "E Tickets," and, at that moment, my "Happiest Place on Earth" was the River Bank, with Rat, Mole, and Badger.

One year later, on a day that started like any other in the 4th grade, I woke up, got dressed, ate breakfast, walked to the John Adams Elementary School, and talked to my friends while we waited for the bell to ring that would beckon us to yet another day in Mrs. Velasco's classroom.

On the new 4th-grade schedule, one did not feel so bludgeoned with heady academia too early in the morning. Before the later hours of the day allotted for Math, English, History, and the like, Mrs. Velasco would warm us up with a nice Reading Hour before our first recess and the onslaught of the perceived meatier subjects.

We were a little more than halfway through a pirate story called "The Ghost in the Noonday Sun." The boy in the story, Oliver Finch, was close to my age, so I vicariously lived the adventures through him. I was not the only one captivated by the exploits of Oliver Finch and his entanglements with the dastardly Captain Scratch, First Mate John Ringrose, Cannibal, and a host of other seafaring reprobates who plundered the Seven Seas. The entire class, both boys and girls, were riveted to this tale as it unfolded on each page, so deliciously read by Mrs. Velasco. She gave different voices to each character, used inflections to their fullest, and had the overall giftedness to take this story right off the pages of the book and plunge it into our fertile imaginations. Even without the occasional turning the book around to parade an illustration in front of us, Mrs. Velasco's oral interpretation breathed life into the characters, the plot, and the setting, making the illustrations a mere backdrop to enhance the story she was already telling so well.

When the bell rang for recess, we were hesitant to go. The bell had been no respecter of the hanging cliff we were on with Oliver Finch and his battle of wits with Captain Scratch. What on any other day would be a sound of emancipation was now a rude awakening to get out and enjoy the sunshine. What was usually characterized by time flying was now interminable. We played the requisite kickball and hopscotch with the other kids in the school, only we were in an incurable state of literary preoccupation.

We stampeded back into our desks after recess with insurrection on our little minds, as Mrs. Velasco took the Math book off her desk and asked us to do likewise.

"Please, Mrs. Velasco—just one more chapter?"

She looked up from the Multiplication Unit staring at her with a look of both surprise and suspicion at our most off-the-wall request.

"Please, Mrs. Velasco, we just have to know if Oliver is going to make it out of this mess!"

Mrs. Velasco looked at each of our faces of great expectations and made the first of a series of decisions at that moment that would fly in the face of the local and state school districts, the Board of Education, the P.T.A., and all of the other official organizations that tenaciously presided over our prescribed curriculum and its dispensation—it would also change my life forever!

After a moment's pause for reflection, Mrs. Velasco closed her Math book.

"Okay, just one more chapter." This was greeted with a rousing "*Thank you! Thank you!*" from her entire 4th-grade class. She gave us a sly, knowing look, as if she were fully aware of our trying to avoid doing any math problems that day. And yet, she also realized that we were in a genuine state of suspense regarding the welfare of Oliver Finch, a state that was in part *her* doing!

One more chapter became two and then three. When an hour had passed, Mrs. Velasco put down "The Ghost in the Noonday Sun" and pulled down a map above the chalk board for our next scheduled lesson. "Okay, class. I want to finish our discussion from yesterday about the mammals in Africa."

The 4th-grade "book addicts" asked the unthinkable, in a direct nose-to-snout confrontation with the elephants, giraffes, lions, and antelope of the Serengeti, who were desiring for us to learn about them.

"Please, Mrs. Velasco—you can't leave us hanging!"

Even though she had obviously read "The Ghost in the Noonday Sun" before, I think Mrs. Velasco had forgotten many of the details in the book and was herself equally in the page-turning mood. The elephants and the lions had to wait.

So did English, History, and a portion of lunch! When the bell rang for us to go home at the end of that momentous day, Mrs. Velasco's class had completely finished reading "The Ghost in the Noonday Sun." No one in the John Adams Elementary School Administration, the Yard Monitors on the playground or the Crossing Guards on the street noticed that 25 students that day were going home with the best education they had ever received to date: the sweet satisfaction that they had visited an incredible world under the dust covers with the explosive knowledge that it was only one in a vast constellation of imaginative places that could be visited with the simple passport known as reading.

The galaxy of characters from these worlds were as fascinating and as varied as the stars in the Milky Way:

Treasure-hunting Long John Silver, man-watching Jo March, monster-making Doctor Frankenstein, ear-exhausting Anne Shirley, world-traveling Phileas Fogg, open-handed Oliver Twist, backfiring Chitty Chitty Bang Bang, ticket-winning Charlie Bucket, home-going Dorothy Gale, ring-bearing Bilbo Baggins, whale-watching Captain Ahab, windmill-searching Don Quixote, vanity-fairing Becky Sharp, panther-following Mowgli, raft-riding Huckleberry Finn, Lilliput-stomping Lemuel Gulliver, case-solving Sherlock Holmes, chocolate-making Willy Wonka, animal-talking Doctor Dolittle, tomorrow-thinking Scarlett O'Hara, lamp-rubbing Aladdin, Friday-finding Robinson Crusoe, sword-wielding Ivanhoe, motorcar-wrecking Mr. Toad, Bounty-mutinying Fletcher Christian, squid-fighting Captain Nemo, rabbit-chasing Alice.

It was my extreme pleasure as a father to take on the responsibility of symbolically handing each of my daughters a large ring of keys that would unlock the doors to these wonderful kingdoms, making books come alive. It was a ring of keys that had been caught (not taught) by me one day when I was 10 years old from Mrs. Velasco.

My tilling of the fertile soil of the two fields of imagination under my cultivating oversight did not stop at a diligent and diverse reading program each night after going upstairs. I also prided myself in surrounding my two daughters with what I call "living illustrations"—whimsical decorations festooning our house as the seasons and holidays rolled along.

Maria would smile and shake her head with hands on her hips in a show of mock disapproval at the eccentricities of her on-the-brink-of-insanity husband. At the same time, she was inwardly beaming at the permanent impression her husband was making on her wide-eyed-with-wonder daughters.

Over the years, our house had won numerous awards bestowed by the City of Monument for our neighborly contribution to the festivity of a particular season. I love to wave the certificates in Maria's face to remind her that I have been validated by a City official as a "professional" in the house-decorating business!!

Our decorating had become so extensive that our Chestnut Street garage's complicated decoration/storage-filing system rivaled the closing scene from *Raiders of the Lost Ark*, where the crated Ark of the Covenant is stored by forklift in a football stadium-sized warehouse, confiscated like all of the other accumulated historical antiquities since the dawn of time that the federal government could possibly get its grubby hands on.

After I had announced that "the time has come!" (to decorate the house again for whatever upcoming season was approaching), Sharayah and Samantha would hop up and gleefully march behind me, filled with gleeful anticipation as I grabbed the ladder and climbed to the appropriate garage cupboard and opened the doors. Inside was a raft of stacked boxes that bore the faded felt-tipped pen designations of "Halloween," "Thanksgiving," "Christmas," "Valentine's Day" and "Easter."

My children would help me carry the daunting army of cardboard boxes back into the house for distribution to the pre-ordained places within our abode. As they grew older, they would even offer their own creative suggestions to help improve the ambiance. As this decorative sophistication began to infect my daughters, I gradually abdicated my creative opinion from time to time, allowing them artistic freedom in the shadow of an occasional artistic difference. Admittedly, the artist in me had to pry the freedom of choice from my clutched hands and grit my teeth as they placed (or misplaced, as the case may be!) some decorative artifact of the season at hand. As my fingers were being proverbially pulled apart, I would admit that I had indeed created this monster. Yet this was father's little dividend for giving my children fuel for their general creativity and to intentionally infuse their imaginations for a specific application and purpose in *reality*.

It was my intention and hope that this cycle of household ornamentation would be an incubator that empowered their faith to be so healthy, and their spiritual discernment so finely tuned, that they would unwaveringly grasp hold of their very real Savior, live an authentic life serving Him, culminating in a real eternity cheering Him.

I have hopefully provided the kindling that can fire Sharayah's and Samantha's imaginations. This has taken the form of pumpkins, Christmas trees, lights, stockings, hearts, and eggs. I have admittedly manufactured bigger-than-life events out of our eccentric decorating in the hopes not only of fostering wonderful childhood memories for my children but also of enhancing their walks with God (who is bigger than life and is busy creating and decorating "in the very beginning" of the Bible!).

So, I have pulled back the string of the bow as far as I can so that the two arrows in my quiver can be shot on a straight-and-narrow trajectory to a bull's-eye presumably farther distant than whatever I may have achieved in my own lifetime.

I remember that one of my own adolescent bowstrings was cut one day when I came home from Monument Junior High School. It was the beginning of my 7th-grade year, and I wanted to take an elective in Music. The Music teacher, Mr. Watson, was a remarkably talented musician who, during our first class, proceeded to demonstrate all variety of brass, wind, string, and percussion instruments with seemingly effortless ability in order for us to properly evaluate which instrument we would like to pursue. Over all of the others, I was captivated by the clarinet. The scope of classical and jazz music it could make with its reedy sounds and the feelings it exuded were fascinating and attractive to me. I snatched up a clarinet case immediately after class, and Mr. Watson gave me a Beginner's Book on the rudiments of this wonderful instrument. My mother was sitting in the family room, knitting some sweater or afghan, when I came barreling into the house after school to announce my newfound instrument of choice. My mother had barely looked up from her knitting, her opinion being formulated the minute she had seen the shape of the black case. "You know, Ian," she said, after I had finished my excited proclamation, "I would much rather hear a trumpet play than a clarinet." It was said so matter of factly, as if she were plainly stating the obvious and it required no additional bravado from her to carry its weight.

She had no idea of her power in that moment as she exchanged her knitting needles for a pair of scissors and cut my bowstring in half. "Well, I'm *still* going to play the clarinet," I stated, with feeble determination. But it was now impossible to shoot the arrow. My attempts at mastering the clarinet in spite of my mother were impeded as I heard the sounds of the trumpet section in class and could see in my mind's eye her nodding in complete approval at the brass sound and conversely grimacing at the clarinet noise I was making by comparison.

I quit the clarinet within a matter of weeks and dropped out of the class.

Consequently, I will protect the bowstrings of my two girls and make sure the tautness is commensurate to the broadening of the imaginative possibilities entertained by them as they begin to realize who they are and can be as daughters of the one, true, almighty God!

I look back on my own creative satisfaction when I discovered that what I could imagine about Christianity was, in fact, *true*! That John 3:16, Philippians 1:6, Ephesians 3:20, and the like are not just cute little verses to be memorized, but boulders of truth quarried from the bedrock of reality by the Spirit-borne-along authors of the Word of God. I remembered my initial divine delight when I discovered that what I had imagined about the Son was actually real! Not only in the receiving *of* the Son but also in the relating *to* the Son for the rest of my earthly life.

This ongoing fact is literally brought home shortly after our house has been transformed into a Yuletide Hallmark Store in early December and I have the opportunity to go upstairs with my two daughters, and we transport ourselves to dark, dreary (and yet somehow beguiling and charming), Dickensian London of 1843 for our traditional reading of *A Christmas Carol*. This is the only Christian-sanctioned "ghost story" I know. At the risk of annual redundancy, I make sure that the admonition from the lips of lamenting, regretful Marley's Ghost is abundantly clear to my girls:

"Why did I walk through crowds of fellow-beings with my eyes turned down, and never raise them to the blessed Star which led the Wise Men to a poor abode!"

A better, opposite example is from little Tiny Tim, who told his father, Bob Cratchit, that "he hoped the people saw him in the church, because he was a cripple, and it might be pleasant for them to remember upon Christmas Day, who made lame beggars walk, and blind men see."

It seems no coincidence to me that the main character's name should be "Ebenezer" Scrooge—his first name alluding to that biblical stone monument commemorating some godly event worth remembering. Upstairs, at Christmastime, I teach my children to learn from those rocks. Read them. Sing them.

> *"Radiant beams from Thy holy face*
> *With the dawn of redeeming grace,*
> *Jesus, Lord at Thy birth,*
> *Jesus, Lord at Thy birth."*

In the Fall, as Halloween gets closer and our house is bedecked with spider webs, scarecrows, and candy corn, and as my children prepare for Trick or Treat and the Fall Carnival at Our Father's Evangelical Church, we traditionally go upstairs each night and read a portion of *The Legend of Sleepy Hollow* by Washington Irving.

Like the fabulously colorful names from Charles Dickens (such as "Fezziwig," "Uriah Heep," and "Artful Dodger"), Washington Irving also captured an equally memorable name for his main character, "Ichabod Crane." I would remind my girls that the name "Ichabod" is actually from the Bible and means "no glory." It calls to mind that old military adage "No guts, no glory!"—which seems very applicable when one thinks of lanky, lazy Ichabod Crane's dabbling in all things superstitious and finally succumbing to them.

His biblical namesake was the grandson of Eli from the Old Testament. Which reminds me of another synopsis I had performed for the "Young and Married" class in a two-part series entitled "The Raising of Children."

Borrowing from the Morleys' first date and my now tried-and-true television themes, I read the synopsis, wearing a neck brace while sitting in a chair that was tipped over on its back. With my feet in the air, I recited,

"Priest Eli is named as a contestant for the 'Father of the Year' game show. His whole family shows up for the television taping as Eli breezes through a series of difficult Old Testament questions, leaving his fellow contestants far behind and dreaming of their 'lovely parting gifts' of Turtle Wax. The live audience is on the edge of their seats as Eli wins his way to the final question for the Grand Prize. You can hear a pin drop as Eli spins the big wheel and is then asked about his own personal fathering skills. At that moment, there are shouts backstage as Eli's sons, Hophni and Phineas, are apprehended by Network Security for attempting to rob the other contestants of their boxes of Turtle Wax as they are leaving. After the scandal, the host decides to disqualify Eli as a potential Grand Prize winner. However, after consulting with the Station Manager, the Network does agree to televise Eli's electric-chair execution due to his rather poor fathering skills.

Please find 1st Samuel, Chapter Two."

Having our daughters was certainly two of the most wonderful events for Maria and me.

Our firstborn's arrival was a bit arduous, however. Maria's water broke one morning in the middle of March (somewhere between the Valentine's Day and Easter decorations), two weeks before her predicted due date. I received the call from Maria at the Block Insurance Agency, swiftly leapt into my Honda

Accord, virtually flew the few blocks up Valentino Avenue to Chestnut Street, and screeched the sedan into our driveway. I was a typical scatterbrained father-to-be. I ran around the house trying to be the embodiment of organization and calm—and manifesting neither. It is amazing that Maria safely made it out the front door, down the driveway, and into our car with me barking stupid suggestions, gathering up unnecessary supplies, and loudly imploring her (with sweat streaming off my brow and panic in my voice) to *"Stay calm!"*

My driving techniques on the short distance to Monument Hospital reflected the same inconsistent desire for Maria's safety while I—channeling audacious amphibian, Mr. Toad—zipped down Valentino Avenue like a bullet, flagrantly ignoring every signal and stop light, arrogantly pronouncing them "out of order" and not nearly as important as the contracting cargo that I was chauffeuring. The screaming blur that was my Honda whipped into the multi-level parking lot of Monument Hospital, ferociously hunting for the closest parking spot to the automatic glass front doors at the entrance. Any other car or pedestrian risked life and limb being in the near vicinity of an insurance agent on a rabid space hunt.

After making a handful of enemies along the way, I finally tracked down a most coveted narrow void between two large sedans. They had not left much room for a car to slide in between them (perhaps they, too, were new-fathers-to-be and had inconsiderately parked this way in haste). Nevertheless, my Honda became a crowbar with a carburetor as I filled up the "pressed down, shaken together" space between the two white lines.

Now, thanks to my squeeze play, the next challenge was to extract the eight-and-a-half-months-pregnant Maria out of the vehicle, with the passenger door's opening capacity being severely diminished by the sedan on the right. Maria's first breathing exercise since our Lamaze classes was to breathe out as deeply as possible to create the illusion of paper thinness and narrowly escape the ridiculously small exit lovingly provided for her by her expedient-to-a-fault husband!

While we were checking in, the grandparents-to-be swooped down upon the lobby, offering their own brand of first-grandchild obnoxiousness. Seth, Nancy, Paulo, and Nicole were all firmly told to take their place in the waiting room by a rather mountainous nurse with whom one would dare not argue. They were not at all pleased with their confinement, but I promised to drop in at every stage of the birthing process. Little did any of us realize that any announcement of a new "chip off the old Block" would not come for another 23 hours!

Maria and I spent the day in our private hospital room, reading contraction monitors and watching the limited channels of the mounted-to-the-ceiling hospital television set. After an epidural released Maria from feeling too much pain, she dropped off into a much-needed sleep late into the night.

Joseph then reported to the Wise Men and shepherds huffing, puffing, and pacing down the hall in the waiting room. I then sought out an empty chair and plopped down myself. Before I, too, fell into a fitful sleep, I suddenly came to the realization that I had not been in these synthetic halls since I had visited my Grandfather Colby for the last time. I was already racked with emotions over the momentous occasion promised by the doctors to be just a few hours away, so I was consequently choked up at the Lord giving and the Lord taking away within the walls of the very same building only a few years apart. I deeply felt the same emotion that had swept over me on our wedding day and wished my four grandparents could have been in the crowded waiting room as well, joining their personalities with the other anxious relatives.

I am sure that my mother, Nancy, was the most apprehensive of the bunch at the soon-to-come offspring of her youngest son, as I myself had almost died at birth. In 1958, yellow jaundice was a life-threatening condition. My brother Owen had been born with a serious level of jaundice, yet it was treatable. Four years later, I came along with an *alarming* level! The doctors told my mother and father that, in all likelihood, I would not make it out of the hospital alive and that they should get used to the idea that they would not ever be able to take me home, let alone risk having any more children! By much obvious prayer from parents and grandparents alike, along with two full blood transfusions and weeks in an incubator, I emerged one morning victorious from the threatening blood disease and was able to be taken home.

"Morning by morning new mercies I see."

Some time the next morning, Owen and Maria's sister Angela arrived at the hospital. I was not available to personally welcome them, as I was now by Maria's side, trying to coach, soothe, encourage, cheer, and "push" Maria toward the imminent conclusion of childbirth. It was far more gut-wrenching than either of us had anticipated. After three hours of pushing and pulling, prodding, screaming, crying, and a useful tool called forceps—prenatal salad tongs—Sharayah Marie Block finally decided it was within her schedule to take a peek at the world!

"It's a girl!" reverberated through the halls of the Maternity Ward of Monument Hospital. The phone lines vibrated with the news as Block family and friends were thus informed.

Maria and I were ecstatic as the nurse placed baby Sharayah Marie into my arms for the first time, and I looked down through tear-filled eyes and whispered, "Hi, sweet girl! We are so glad to see you. You are so beautiful! Welcome to your new home!" I pulled out a ring of colorful plastic keys and softly rattled them in front of her. Maria shook her head and smiled in amused tolerance at my impetuousness when I then asked my new baby daughter, "Now, Sharayah, what would you like to read first?"

Samantha Nicole Block joined our familial ranks four years later one morning early in February (between the Christmas and Valentine's Day decorations). The same cast of characters stormed Monument Hospital: Seth, Nancy, Paulo, and Nicole absently pawing through inane magazines in the waiting room, and I, pep-talking Maria through another labor. Samantha, however, decided not to give us nearly the suspense that Sharayah had inflicted; she made her debut after only eight hours of "encouragement."

When Samantha was placed in my arms, I tearfully greeted her in kind and pulled out the same old plastic ring of keys, pitted and marred from Sharayah's teething four years earlier, giving her the same premature invitation "Now, Samantha, what would you like to read first?"

We have been turning pages ever since.

This constant exposure to the written word over time has been the cause of a surprisingly expansive vocabulary for all of us. Juicy, three-dollar words and phrases seem to crop up in our writing and speaking as spontaneously as a sesquipedalian belch that erupts after a heavy meal of highbrow literature and its necessary partner, the dictionary! I laugh sometimes at my girls using words far beyond their "normal" vocabulary. I have to catch myself, as well, from getting too carried away with the not-at-all-extinct giant Thesaurus stomping around and roaring from its linguistic lungs the multi-syllabic words in my head.

Now, I know that raising kids is more than reading and decorating. It is trench warfare that includes everything from drooling to Driver's Training, pacifiers to peer pressure, diapers to dating, measles to marriage.

And to properly navigate these weighty caterpillar-to-butterfly transitions, a parent must be the living, eating, breathing synonym of integrity. That "word is your bond," "mean what you say" personality trait that is as reliable as Earth's rotation, as consequential as gravity. Sharayah learned this indelibly of her father one night after going upstairs.

The stuffed turtle was named Shelley. It was a gift from her grandparents. Sharayah's singular infatuation for the fuzzy little reptile that was oddly blue was nothing short of bottom-of-the-heart adoration. It all started with our nightly bedtime game of "Tickle War." Not the most intelligent prescription for calming before sleep, but a lot of fun, nonetheless.

The "war" was winding down for the night, with peace treaties ready to be signed and "goodnight" ready to be gently said, when Sharayah decided on one last provocation, hauling off and hitting me on the head with Shelley. She laughed uproariously. And since the assault provided her with such side-splitting enjoyment, she did it again. After the turtle had crashed down upon my head for the third time, I told Sharayah that that was quite enough. With "Tickle War" adrenaline still refusing to subside in her, she heard nary a word of my warning as she pounded me again with the floppy, compliant Shelley. I ramped up my seriousness with, "Okay, Sharayah, it's time to stop!" *Wham!* was Shelley's answer, along with a big, broad sinister smile across Sharayah's face. It was then that I laid down the gauntlet.

"If you hit me one more time with that turtle, I am going to throw it out the window!" Now I know that sometimes exasperated parents make disciplinary threats to their children that they can't possibly keep. The fight for compliance with their authority starts off simple enough, with perhaps "no dessert" after dinner, but can quickly escalate into "canceling Christmas" before you know it. But whether a sundae or Santa is now held in the balance, your integrity is always on the line.

Upon hearing my words, Sharayah's eyes widened in awe-struck astonishment, but her raised eyebrows betrayed suspicion, while her pursed lips guarded a playful curiosity that has been the death wish of many a cat. You could see that she was wrestling with the remote possibility of my actually following through on such an audacious action. Her answer was Shelley, once again, slamming down upon my head—only this time the unsuspecting turtle was snatched out of Sharayah's grip with the lightning speed of a parental paw!

I very calmly rolled out of her bed, turtle in hand. While exhaled gasps of disbelief were chugging from my now-panicked older daughter, I walked over to the window, raised the shade, turned the latch, pried open the screen, and pitched the plush toy right out of the two-story window and into the darkness. There was silence. For one, because stuffed animals don't make a sound when they hit the ground, but also because Sharayah was momentarily speechless, but only momentarily.

Recovering from the stunning fact that I had just performed what was promised, she shot out of the bed yelling, "Shelley!" like the cavalry was coming to the rescue. In a pink pajama blur, she ran out of the bedroom, down the stairs, through the kitchen, and out the back door when her eyes beheld the spot where the stuffed turtle lay in a disheveled heap, shell-shocked.

Breathless, Sharayah eventually returned to her bedroom, gently cradling the limp creature with life-and-death delicacy. Ignoring me, she carefully placed the turtle head tenderly on her pillow, covering the little blue body with a blanket up to its leathery blue neck. The button turtle eyes stared at me blankly, while its expressionless turtle mouth gave no sign of affection toward me.

Even so, Shelley and I never butted heads again.

Amidst all of this inherent child-rearing chaos is the undaunted parental quest to implant a personal desire in each child to adhere himself or herself to the true faith, receiving the Author and Perfecter personally, and then, with eyes fixed, hanging onto their seats for the ride of their lives.

Maria and I have tried our best to train up our two daughters in the way they should individually go, so they never would even consider departing from it, as that would mean departing from *Him*. To the extent that this is not even an option for them, we relax. Even so, the process of rearing children is still a real nail-biter.

I am sure there was just as much nail-biting in eternity when the Children of Israel gave their Heavenly Father a run for his manna by consistently trying his Divine patience. Is it any wonder that their collective national name never graduated to something more mature? They never became the Adolescents of Israel, or even the Adults of Israel. Remarkably, the Children of Israel they would always remain, and the Bible is abundantly clear as to why.

There is much that is sobering about the Israelites' exhaustive struggle to get *their* way with *Yahweh*. For the second part of my series on "The Raising of Children," I borrowed an orange prison jumpsuit from a member of Our Father's Evangelical Church who worked for the Los Angeles County Sheriff's Department, complete with a block of identification numbers across the back. The "Young and Married" class was predictably taken aback at seeing their teacher dressed in this way. It only made sense when I walked up to the podium of our room in the Educational Christianity building and read,

> "Fathers Jeroboam and Rehoboam each live on the North and South end of a block in a poorly planned subdivision of tract homes. Neither can manage their households very well. Their children are out of control. Major and Minor Prophets attempt to babysit each household on numerous occasions but cannot get the undisciplined children to listen. The babysitters are finally forced to call the Father on their phones. As a result, the Assyrian Social Services invade Jeroboam's home on the northern end of the block and cart off the children by force to the 'Stop Your Whining Detention Camp' in the North. Later, the Babylonian Social Services storm the home of Rehoboam on the south end of the block and drag the children off to the 'I Told You So Correctional Facility' in the South.

> *Open your Bibles, please, to 2nd Kings, Chapter Seventeen."*

My take on all of this: better to have the book *read* to you than have the book *thrown* at you!

Which takes me right back upstairs with my daughters as I read nightly to them not only from the Providential perspectives found in the great classics of literature, but from the Supreme Center of the literary universe as well. Is it any wonder that the Apostle John started his gospel with only a "Word" and ended

20 chapters later with a gigantic library? And this was no typical floor-to-ceiling, manly mahogany library, complete with rolltop desk, cigar smoke, and a spinning old world globe—this library *was* the globe! Every other book in the universe of print—children's nursery rhymes, adventure classics, poetry, pulp novels, biographies, Christian self-help—were all swept off the shelves to make room for *one* book with *one* central character. Once that life was recorded for all eternity, there was no more room!

There was no more need.

Taking my cues from the Apostle John, I opened Samantha's Children's Bible one night in November (between the Halloween and Thanksgiving decorations), and asked her what story she would like to read that night. Samantha is becoming the consummate animal lover (following in the footsteps of "Rabbit Killer" Paula Henson). She loves to hear the Creation account and the vast populations of animals popping into existence by the vocal brush strokes of the Great Zookeeper. Her Bible is filled with attractive, whimsical, exaggerated depictions of those eventful six days, so she is a captive audience again and again.

"Okay," I sighed in anticipatory doldrums at the monotony of reading this requested story for the umpteenth time.

"In the Beginning . . ."

"No, Daddy!"

"What?"

"You know how we start a story!"

"Oh, that's right." I realized that Samantha required that same starting-gate pronouncement that Sharayah had over so many years of our reading together.

No matter *what* the book or story, I was required to interject this particular line of commencement. I smiled at Samantha's waiting face. To begin the creation account in this unique way was agreeable to me because both Sharayah and Samantha now had a very good grasp on the difference between fact and fiction, reality and fantasy. I pondered for a moment before I spoke again, thinking in split-second intervals of the innumerable reasons why the Bible is not only *the* Good Book, but *a* good book as well!

There are . . .

. . . dungeons and dragons, wrong gods and wet fleeces, mysterious shadows creeping up and down stairs, witches from Endor, sorcerers from Cyprus, fortune tellers from Philippi, giants from Gath—even bigger ones from Bashan—martyrs and madmen, rich fools, poor sages, shipwrecks, marauding desert pirates, tent-peg head murders, heads on silver platters, piles of male body parts, blood as deep as horse heads, vomiting fish, raven waiters, cowardly lions, bears mauling teenagers, sweet-talking serpents, demon-possessed pigs, fall-out from heaven, flaming arrows from Hell, blinding barbers, burning emperors from Rome, handwashing governors from Judea, curious queens from Sheba, courageous queens from Persia, conniving queens thrown from windows, arks made into covenants, prisoners made into princes, princes made into patriarchs, patriarchs spared at the altar—*and* fooled at the altar—shepherds made into kings, kings turned into hairy monsters, red-hairy brothers turned into outcasts, a prophet who marries a whore, a whore who protects an army, a baby out of wedlock who becomes a Savior . . .

"Okay." I returned from my reverie to Samantha's seven-year-old room and to the Children's Bible in my lap opened to Page One.

"Are you ready?" I asked.

"Yes!" she responded excitedly.

"Once Upon a Time . . ."

CHAPTER SEVEN

HE'S IN HIS PULPIT . . .

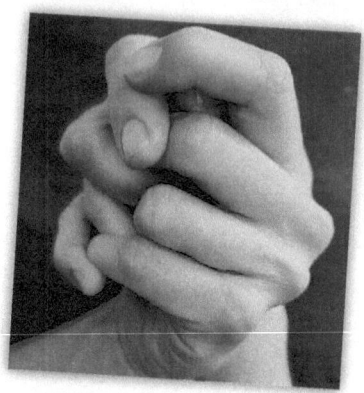

"We peep into the Gospel only on the eve of making speeches, in order to dazzle the audience by our acquaintance with what is, anyway, a rather original composition, which may be used to produce a certain effect—all to serve the purpose! But what Christ commands is something very different."
—FYODOR DOSTOEVSKY, *The Brothers Karamazov*

I have always resented the term "bully pulpit." I hope, as far as it concerns me, that the term is only an oxymoron. *Anyone* who would use the platform intended for the illuminating of Holy Scripture for their own self-seeking purposes would most certainly fall under the category of "moronic ox."

Whenever a bully was confronted on the playground at the John Adams Elementary School, caught in the act of oppressing someone usually diminutive in stature and ability, the exhortation from the disgusted crowd of onlooking children would be for him to "pick on someone your own size!"

But the bully can only see in a mirror dimly. He does not anticipate one day being fully known. If so, he would be terrified at the imminent selection of a candidate to pick on that is *exactly* one's own size—oneself! Only then is the size an absolutely perfect match.

Prior to any biblical lesson or sermon, the first person who needs a good talkin' to is the one *behind* the pulpit! This preparation safeguards a potential bully from replacing a true mouthpiece of God.

Over the years, I have been blessed (and consequently eligible for stricter judgment) by being able to teach adults at the now- flourishing Our Father's Evangelical Church in a variety of venues. Our growing church was riding the crest of a wave under the pastoral leadership of Milton Derringer. After the initial years of resistance to change, the Body of Christ at the corners of Ridgeway and Valentino Avenues fell in step with the spiritual calisthenics counted out by Sheriff Derringer. As a result, blood pressures were lowered, thinking was clearer, muscles were toned, and fat was trimmed. I relished opening the Word of God each Sunday under these prolific circumstances.

Like a four-pronged fork in my road of life, I have distilled certain subjects as "pets" of mine. Their themes keep recurring in both subtle and overt ways in my teaching. I have found these four "pulpits" to have evolved over the years as my life has slipped by and midlife lurks around the corner. However,

I am careful to make sure I have given myself a good talkin'
to before anyone within earshot hears what I have to say on
the subjects.

The first of these mini-sermon prongs is . . .

Virginity

"'She is not my mistress,' replied the young sailor gravely,
'she is my betrothed.'

'Sometimes one and the same thing,' said Morrell,
with a smile.

'Not with us, sir,' replied Dantes.'"
—ALEXANDRE DUMAS, *The Count of Monte Cristo*

Maria and I had maintained our virginity until we were
married. We made these preliminary vows separately between
God and ourselves. We were not even friends at the time, but
we utilized the same source of strength and endurance to hold
up the standard bar. We each had a resolve of the flesh not to
do something physically Wrong that would one day adversely
affect Mr. or Mrs. Right. Our hormones, like termites, would
have eaten our purity attempts alive if our abstinence did not
resiliently hang on to the omnipotent Holy Spirit, who had sentry
duty around our individual temples. Only then were we capable
of locking horns with the alluring temptations that screamed
for our attention and made our skin crawl:

"No one needs to know—it will be our little secret!"
"It will feel great—trust me!"
"But I love you so much!"
"We're going to get married soon, anyway!"

By the time Maria and I had finally reached the altar, after many different girlfriends and boyfriends, from first kiss to making out, from first date to senior proms, we had protected our virginity only by the miraculous exterminating power of God, who kept the termites of temptation at bay.

One night, the lifelong plot to kidnap and murder my virginity finally reached a level of intensity so desperate as to risk overexposure. The mythological siren in this case was a girlfriend that I was seriously dating while attending junior college. She had invited me over for dinner at the apartment she was sharing with her sister and brother-in-law while going to school. Home-made enchiladas were the draw, along with an empty house, thanks to a coincidental "date night" for her sister and brother-in-law. Upon my arrival, she handed me a Coke, my beverage of choice. The food was still cooking, so we sat on the couch and passed the time "innocently" making out. One thing led to another, and she was soon lying down on top of me, her hands beginning to rove like metal detectors on a sensual beach. A strange lightheadedness was coming over me, a foreign, unnatural relaxation and dizzy euphoria. She could feel my uneasiness at the new sensations and slyly whispered in my ear while kissing my neck, "I put rum in your Coke." Not unexpectedly, the alcohol was having a field day in someone who doesn't drink. In spite of the growing numbness, however, internal alarms were still going off, alerting a potential sexual free-fall. It was enough to capture back a split-second of sobriety. I gently grabbed her shoulders and moved her off of me while I endeavored to clumsily sit up. "I need to leave," I said both frankly and apologetically. She was at once surprised and peeved. I walked out of the apartment—the cool night air helping to regain my senses—got in my car, and drove the short distance back home. Whatever risk was involved being briefly behind the wheel under some influence seemed at the time to pale in comparison to potentially permanent moral damage over enchiladas.

Not exactly a cloak-sacrificing, mad-dash escape from the nagging clutches of Potiphar's wife, but it was close enough!

Our wedding night was a passion no-hitter. This was partly due to unspoken, nervous stalling, and also a chunk of good old-fashioned fatigue after a long wedding day and a "party all night long!" reception. On the second night of our honeymoon (in spite of six months of marriage counseling by Pastor Finch and a romantic drive up the coast of California to enhance the mood), we were still laughably ignorant about everything you always wanted to know about sex.

The second night's consummation attempt was more exploratory in nature. Only I was Christopher Columbus, and Maria was the West Indies! As soon as the *Nina*, the *Pinta*, and *Santa Maria* sighted the shoreline, I dropped the anchors before the tide pulled the ships in and crashed them on the rocks. I waved my national flag from the helm.

"Maria."

"Huh?" My spoken word had startled her from her physical preoccupation.

"What, what is it?" She was slightly surprised and alarmed.

"Uh . . ." for lack of a better way to phrase it, I continued guiltily, "you need to sin with me!" It was the best way I could communicate my feelings. She needed to pick up a shovel and take part in the ground-breaking ceremony!

Only hours before, our current behavior would have been violent vandalism to our temples of the Holy Spirit. Now, it was a congratulations graduation "Block" party with enticing food and surprises in every room, and I was overwhelmed! Maria understood my trepidation immediately and sent out welcoming shore parties to which, at first sight, I hoisted the anchors.

I used to think that Maria and I were quixotic dinosaurs in an era of pre-marital everything as we quietly enjoyed the spectacular physical blessings and benefits of waiting. I have since wised up and begun proclaiming what has never been outdated from the rooftops: *drinking from my own cistern solely with the wife of my youth!*

I also pray for the same spiritual invasion of privacy that compelled Maria and me to also befall my two daughters, as well as the boys and men who befriend them, and eventually marry them. May they be equally empowered to patrol and protect their purity.

The Apostle Paul's correspondence to the church in Philippi is a joyful enigma. True, he was instrumental in saving a jailor and his family as well as a purple fashion designer. But he also suffered severe beatings and cruel imprisonment. Still, he promises at the outset of his letter that the Faithful One will complete the good work begun in you. You can take that all the way to the bank! In the meantime, Paul reiterates later, you have unlimited assets as you can do all things through Christ who gives you strength.

And, last I checked, "virginity" is still on that list!

Politics

"The Queen turned crimson with fury, and, after glaring
at her for a moment like a wild beast, began screaming,
  'Off with her head! Off—'
'Nonsense!' said Alice, very loudly and decidedly,
and the Queen was silent."
                    —LEWIS CARROLL, *Alice in Wonderland*

During my first three years on the Deacon Board at Our Father's Evangelical Church, I would hear the criticisms raised from time to time that Pastor Milton Derringer was *too* political!

Some of these opinions were expressed as mere observations, while others were acerbic, with personal offense. His response to me when I forwarded these messages to him was a surprising "On the contrary, Ian, I don't think I am political enough!"

Ever since Virgil Cronklin had panicked me as a child after the showing of *For I Am Not Ashamed*, I was acutely interested in the political machinations of America. I had a chance to ask Pastor Derringer about his views one day at the Rush More Coffee House. The restaurant was only a few blocks down the hill from the church on Mountain View Drive, so it is a popular watering hole for the O.F.E. membership. It derives its clever name from not only its rapid service—of which it is proud—but also for the excellent view of Rudolph Valentino it affords on the booths lining the plate glass window at the back of the restaurant, thereby reminding customers of the monument's original inspiration over 1,000 miles to the northeast.

Only Rudolph was looking more like Vincent van Gogh with a towel on his head these days, as a good portion of his left ear fell off during the January 1994 California-Northridge earthquake. The ear slid down the mountainside and came to a stop only a couple hundred feet away from the face, so it remains visible from the town. Now the monument really does resemble the insane artist in mid-razor battle with his so-called "friend" and fellow artist, Paul Gauguin.

Old movie star buff Max Stellar would have regretted the convoluted impressions his creation was now making. Not only were the glory days of film-making depicted, but also ancient

Egypt, and now an eccentric artist all commemorated in one famous half-face.

Pastor Derringer and I were seated right next to the same booth in the back of the restaurant where we had sat three years before during my first deacon interview with him after the Samuel Caldwell desertion. It was now November, election time, so the subject I was broaching was ripe.

"You were criticized again for your political statements last Sunday, Milton."

"Oh?" Milton's interest was piqued.

"Yeah, Sara Pollard and Fred Sanchez both came up to me and expressed their discomfort at your political incorrectness."

"Let me guess," he smiled knowingly, "it was my conclusions about the Old Testament's School of the Prophets, right?"

"Yes." Pastor Derringer was in the middle of an Old Testament survey on Sunday mornings, and he'd made some observations regarding the School of the Prophets—whose Major and Minor alumni not only populated the writings of the Old Testament, but they also physically occupied and affected the Middle Eastern regions all the way up to the highest levels of the political culture of their day.

"The criticism comes as no surprise, Ian. For some reason, certain people don't like to hear about the political influence of the people of God in the Old Testament. They think I'm politicizing the pulpit when, in reality, I'm just rendering the political facts of life as they are found in Scripture."

"But Pastor, the Nation of Israel is not a very good example for us in the United States, is it?" For the most part, I would agree with Pastor Derringer's perspective on these issues to the extent that I could clarify and weigh what he had to say during this chat over lunch.

"It was a *theocracy*, Ian, a historically unique 'government by God,' and yet—"

"Gentlemen, are you ready to order?"

Our waiter, George, had sidled up to our table and interrupted our conversation (that would have obviously gone for days on end without nourishment unless George had made his presence known).

We gave him our lunch orders. Mine was the same club sandwich, a routine lunch meal I ordered virtually every time I dined at the Rush More Coffee House.

When George had left to place our order, Milton continued.

"The Nation of Israel's influence spilled over to the likes of Nebuchadnezzar, Darius, Xerxes, the Queen of Sheba, Herod, Nero, Caligula. For good or ill, Ian, they all had to contend with the people of God."

"So you think we should have the same influence in our modern-day society? I mean, wasn't that all Old Testament politics? Didn't Jesus change all that by telling us to be more passive?"

Milton paused for a minute, absently looking through the window up at the face of Rudolph. He was apparently searching for something germane to the conversation that was stored in his mind. "Where I come from, in Washington State," he resumed, "you drive by hundreds of lush apple orchards. Every time I would look out at the rows and rows of delicious red apples, I would try to assess and re-assess how well I was doing with the nine 'fruit slices' of the Spirit. Some would like to confuse the one named 'peace,' which made the final cut, with 'passivity,' which absolutely did not!"

As he had an appointment scheduled shortly after our lunch, Milton dove right in when our food arrived. While I was busy garnishing my club sandwich, he digressed a bit by launching into one of his many non-pastoral aspirations. "You know, Ian, if I had not been called to be a pastor, I think I would have liked to be an author. I have this great idea for a sort of science fiction-political thriller book, where all of a sudden, by some cosmic force, all of the original Founding Fathers appear walking the streets of downtown Washington, D.C. Imagine bumping into Thomas Jefferson on the steps of the Capitol, or better yet, standing under the Washington Monument with George himself!"

He paused to chew his food. He was too excited about his "pipe dream" to fully clear his mouth as he continued, "The climax of the story is a nationally televised debate between the Founding Fathers, who have now gathered together, and the leaders of the A.C.L.U., taking place in either the House or Senate chambers at the Capitol. The debate that would ensue could be a marvelous exercise in how far we have deteriorated!"

"Sounds great," I said as a buffer to return to our original discussion. "But what about all that 'giving to Caesar what is Caesar's'?"

"What about it?" Milton said between chews, a bit disappointed that his novel dream discussion did not progress any further.

"Well, it sounds like Jesus is shrugging his shoulders at the government."

"It was easier *then* to understand Him."

"How so?"

"It was a Roman dictatorship. You gave back to the government what they were demanding. You can't pass off your responsibilities so easily now."

"What do you mean?"

"Have you ever heard of 'government *of* the people, *by* the people and *for* the people'?"

"Yeah, so?"

"So, the government, is *you*, Ian. *Now* giving back to Caesar is you and I dutifully giving back to *ourselves* by taking the responsibility of being politically involved and concerned. A great opportunity to be salt and light if there ever was one!"

"That doesn't seem to go over so well at O.F.E."

"I wish we could shed those conversational taboos of not ever being able to discuss religion and politics among ourselves. We are so worried about potential disagreements and possible disunity that the mere mention of politics from the pulpit makes people bristle."

"Some people think you're an activist."

"I should hope not!" Milton looked around and flagged down our waiter. "Check please!" he called and then looked back at me.

"To me, activists are those angry, stodgy curmudgeons who picket and boycott anything and everything offensive to them. They are far too reactionary for me."

"So what does that make you?"

"Well, proactive, I hope! By my constant (and hopefully gracious), responsible involvement in political issues as a tax-paying, voting Christian citizen, I don't have to react to anything because I am not caught by surprise. You can be awfully cranky when you're suddenly awakened from a deep sleep, Ian! My alertness to issues, coupled with the Holy Spirit's tongue motivation and control, along with a resigned awareness of the overall sovereignty of God, keeps me from being caught off-guard or too disappointed by some sad turn of events. After all, *I'm just passin' through*, as they say. And speaking of just passin' through, I need to leave!"

With much to chew on even after lunch, I walked with Milton up to the cash register at the front of the restaurant. Milton graciously paid our bill and took the change in his hands. He then counted off three $1 bills and said to me, "Here, Ian—go give these to George."

I nodded and trotted back to our table, which was in the process of being bused. I then noticed that Milton had already left a generous tip on the table!

I stood there, puzzled. I casually looked down at the face pictured on the three bills in my hand and finally got the joke.

I looked across the restaurant to see Milton smiling at "*me* the people."

"Very funny!" I muttered.

Tithing

"'Next,' said the captain, 'I learn we are going after treasure—hear it from my own hands, mind you. Now treasure is ticklish work; I don't like treasure voyages on any account, and I don't like them, above all, when they are secret.'"
—ROBERT LOUIS STEVENSON, *Treasure Island*

My first tithe was stolen money that I would clandestinely pilfer from a ceramic, coiled snake coin holder on the top of Owen's desk each Sunday morning after I had snuck into his room while he was taking a shower. This "Robin Hood" method was more kleptomaniacal than it was biblical. Mountebank or not, at least this criminal giving pattern indicated an awareness on my part of a scriptural mandate and an innate compulsion to comply.

As I grew older, my giving became more law-abiding. That one-tenth, first-fruits-off-the-top became my standard for all monies, whether pittance or windfalls, that came my way. Once this obligatory generosity reached habit level, it became more genuine and less confined to the original "10% Paradigm." Ten percent became 20, then 30, then 40, to the point where I no longer bothered to calculate lest I fall into the trap—which money can often produce—of acting like I'm in some sort of spiritual contest flinging money toward heaven as a down payment on a nice, bejeweled crown, sparkling tiaras for my wife and daughters, a castle in the air, and rooms with a view.

On the contrary, my life with God's hand in my pocketbook has been an exhilarating exercise in financial freedom. I can look back on my swelling offerings over the years and observe His thorough, proportionate compensation and care in all of the compartments that make up my life.

What is fascinating to me is that, although there is a formidable body of evidence pointing to the ongoing sustenance of God, at first glance, it seems circumstantial at best. There are no check-and-balance formulas that can be calculated in order to determine the exact fiscal year-end profits and losses of the Divine Corporation and its earthly stockholders. The C.E.O. does not operate that way.

The issue of *faith* convolutes any attempt at hard-and-fast bookkeeping. But what faith's hindsight does point to, however, is an ever-increasing stack of tangential evidence suspiciously related to the practice of cheerful giving. The pile of testimonials from myself and my family undeniably point to the direct provisions of God: rescue after rescue—financial and otherwise, supernatural strength not present moments before, sudden peace prevailing over anguish and angst, a specifically qualified individual walking into our lives with advice and ability perfectly able to guide and direct when we had not a clue, the discovery of a Bible verse or passage we so desperately needed to hang our hats on, and, yes, the roof-over-our-heads, clothes-on-our-backs, and food-on-the-table issues that are methodically, routinely maintained by an unseen Hand.

So, the evidence is indeed profound, even obvious. The faith view looking back is crystal clear. These are *not* thick files of unrelated coincidences—there are just too many! Unless one wants to subscribe to a financial Big Bang theory, the Owner of the cattle on a thousand hills is very much alive and well!

I have often marveled at this phenomenon. True, we are blessed with the temporal blessings of house, car, and job. But we are growing more confident that the issue is not in the provisions but in the *Provider.* Circumstances may change dramatically, in an instant, whether they be financial, health, or even a season of spiritual depravity. Through it all, is the giver still cheerful, even hilarious? Confident in the C.E.O.? To answer that question, one must put the calculator back in the drawer and measure one's faith instead!

Maria and I are of the mindset that we should give solely and generously to our local church. After all, it is the modern-day prototype of the *only* institution found in the Acts of the Apostles that was designated to implement, by the collective contributions of its membership: *flourishing* local ministries as they are needed, the propulsion of the Message on a worldwide scale unhindered, with an *abundant* supply of monetary ammunition for ever-expanding mission fields, as well as supplying the *personal* needs of the missionaries who cultivate them.

Each year, my accountant in Monument has the same reaction when preparing my tax returns. He is an extremely efficient, competent, and capable C.P.A. He is also an atheist.

"I don't know how you do it, Ian!" He would chuckle as he shakes his head with disbelief at what he calls the reckless amount filled in under the "Charitable Contributions" tax-deduction category designated to Our Father's Evangelical Church, while he simultaneously admits that it has all worked itself out . . . again!

I suppose I should invite him to lunch one day and somehow cram the gospel into our conversation or give him an appropriately subtle book on the rudiments of my faith, or invite him to a non-threatening, good-news-sneaking O.F.E. outreach event. In the meantime, however, his comatose spirit is perplexed when he looks down at my tax return and sees not just all talk (I guess I have put my money where my mouth is), but the bones and sinews of a faith that is undeniably working—year after year after year.

God loves not only the cheerful giver, but the chortling atheist as well!

What is maddening to Maria and me is the closet of fiduciary secrecy to which tithing has been relegated by the local church. We both wonder how the church can communicate at so many important levels, even intrude in one another's intimate lives all under the pretense of "accountability": carnality, incest, abortion, adultery, sinful thoughts, stealing on the job are all fodder for the evangelical confessional. But dare to ask someone about the consistency of their tithing, and you might as well have performed an unwanted autopsy on their soul, prematurely removing all vital organs! Not only does the right hand not know what the left hand is doing, it is none of your business no matter *what* they're doing—or *not* doing, as the case may be!

One of the offspring of the Father of Fibs is the barricade of secrecy around one's checkbook and the prevention of any observation as to its allocations in the Treasure-Heart-Ratio Department. I have continued to be a reckless giver, according to the criteria of my C.P.A. I am always mindful that I do not want my earthly barns to become too full with superfluous grain.

As a result, my heart looks forward to a many-mansioned eternity, full of prepared places in which we will forever dwell. Although, I wonder if my heavenly home will have an extra guest house that was built with Owen's money!

Reconciliation

"'The greatest happiness for a man is the conquest of himself; and that, O prince, is what I have to ask of you.' She spoke rapidly, and with animation; indeed, she never appeared to him so fascinating. 'You had once a friend,' she continued.

'It was in your boyhood. There was a quarrel, and you and he became enemies. He did you wrong. After many years, you met him again in the Circus at Antioch.'

'Messala!'

'Yes, Messala.

'You are his creditor. Forgive the past; admit him to friendship again; restore the fortune he lost in the great wager; rescue him.'"

—LEW WALLACE, *Ben-Hur*

Lorne and Candice Carlson were our very best friends. Maria and I met them at Our Father's Evangelical Church shortly after we were married and they were engaged.

After the Carlsons were married, our relationship continued to grow into a very close foursome, rooted in bonds of love that sank deeper and deeper as the years rolled by.

And then, all Hell broke loose.

Well, at least a big chunk of it broke off from the main hive and dispatched a deliberate demonic meteor shower to pelt the soul of target Block. In my 37 years of life, I have never experienced such forces of darkness as this before. Nor did I see the snarling detachment coming. The rapacious attack came out of a clear-blue spiritual sky and caught me completely unawares. The first pincer from the Pit clamped around my self-image and whispered into my spirit's ear,

"You're not qualified or worthy to be a deacon at your church. If any of your fellow deacons had the slightest idea what went on in that carnal head of yours, they would ride you out on a rail!"

The hot breath cauterized my logic, and I became a captive audience to the intensified whispers as the case against me grew more accusatory.

"You have no business teaching the Bible in *any* capacity to anyone at the church, as that privilege should be reserved only for those with *'A Closer Walk With Thee'!*"

It is fascinating how believable the netherworld can be when they have a strategy to take you down. They merely play upon your weaknesses and exaggerate them into a mental state of spiritual disqualification. All the while, this self-esteem collapse pummeled my central nervous system with headaches, nausea, lack of appetite, and a growing deliberate aloofness from those around me. It was not the hard knocks from the school of life that was showing up in my pale, gaunt face (highlighted with lengthening crow's feet and new wrinkles), but rather the etchings from the sucking vortex of the school of slow death.

As my separation became more and more distant, one demon got down on all fours behind my back where I was shakily standing while another distracted me with the prosecution's closing argument:

"Ian Block, you are *so* unqualified for Christianity. You are living a lie within your own family! They would be so much better off without you—at least they would not have such a hypocritical example to follow. Why don't you just end it all and give them some welcome relief?"

After weeks of hellish harassment, this last line was fed to me one Saturday while I was mowing my lawn. The whispering demon then tried to push me over the back of the demon crouching behind me so that I would topple over and permanently fall out of the army of God. I had to literally shake my head to expel the thoughts; I walked into our house in mid-mow to alert Maria that my attackers were back. I was ashamed that I had let them into my house by way of myself, but there had not been even a hint that they were on the move toward our house on Chestnut Street.

I was also becoming numb to prayers, Scripture, and the continuously suggested self-help books.

Not too many people were privy to my condition, as we thought they might misconstrue my struggle as some ultimate form of demonic possession, making me the Linda Blair of 1995. I reported to a few close friends who came alongside me in order to deflect the abysmal assertions and to rescue my battered soul. Foremost in this group was, of course, the Carlsons. Their role had a price to pay, however, as I took out my confusion and scorn on Lorne. I tested him, clung to him, pushed him away, taunted him, smothered him, and shunned him again. All in a vain, flailing attempt to get a grip on what was happening.

I finally accused them both of an underhanded betrayal of my confidence to someone outside our agreed circle of confidants. The communication leak was true; their intentions, however, were to gain further insight into my condition and to fortify their own coping in the process. I saw this as egregious gossip and accused them of such, as the "Principalities and Powers" siege engines roared at me for nearly three months. Our friendship with the Carlsons could not handle the pressure and finally cracked and shattered under the weight of my inadvertent brutality.

By now the faces of Maria and those around me were also showing signs of wear and tear. It was then that the "greater is He that is in me" defending army of all I knew to be true—as far back as the simple lessons of Mrs. Hawkins—routed my darkness with a flash of light that was just as sudden as the enemy's initial attack. This offered me an incandescent moment when I finally spotted the snuffing-out strategy for what it was as the hired killers of evil grew cocky and pushed too far, too soon. My sudden "Ah-hah!" moment produced the very result described by Martin Luther:

"The best way to drive out the devil, if he will not yield to the texts of Scripture, is to jeer and flout him, for he cannot bear scorn."

The moment I had caught a brief glimpse of their odious battle plans and saw them for what they were, they quickly rolled up their maps, struck down their tents, and slithered off into the bushes, prowling around in their best lion imitations, looking for another sap that would not see them coming, and yet another maggot feeding-frenzy would commence, ravaging more carcasses of spiritual warfare.

I had two casualties of war from my three-month-long ordeal: Lorne and Candice Carlson. The hurt and pain that had been inflicted upon them scarred and maimed our once-precious friendship. We bitterly tore ourselves from each other, never to be close friends again.

Though we co-existed at Our Father's Evangelical Church, we only maintained a level of civility so as not to arouse suspicion among others who knew of our previous friendship.

Our separation was artful. Four wronged brothers and sisters erroneously attempting to sincerely worship at O.F.E. without the slightest thought of making things right beforehand. This division and separation continued as the glowing embers from our previous battle kept our memories still hot under the collar.

We even pasted and glued the jagged rip between us with *other* friends and busied ourselves with *other* activities that would aid us in getting on with our lives. We got on for two long years, until *God* said, "Ah-hah!"—not that He needed to suddenly discover that something was amiss (He obviously would have known that all along!). It was just His perfect timing to show Himself at a moment when it was only Himself who could possibly get the credit for what was about to happen.

Once again, I did not see this coming, as it was Saturday, and I was busy mowing my lawn!

Like the voice on the hilltop at the Cheyenne Christian Conference Center, my second "theophany" was authoritative yet friendly, inaudible yet distinct, gentle yet to the point.

"Ian, you need to ask for forgiveness from Lorne and Candice Carlson for what *you* did to them."

Before I could offer a rebuttal from my side of the hurt fence, the Heavenly Father lit the fuse of my teaching memories—from Jacob and Esau, the Prodigal Son, to the Cross—and I was rendered speechless.

In perfect clarity after two long years, I saw my sole responsibility—I had singlehandedly dragged our friendship with the Carlsons to Hell and back.

Standing on the front lawn, I nodded my head to no one in particular and, once again in mid-mow, went straight into the house to inform Maria of my God-given intentions. She was upstairs in our bathroom, brushing her hair. I stood in the doorway, caked in dust and grass stains, and blurted out, "I need to ask Lorne and Candice to forgive me."

Maria dropped both brush and jaw.

She looked at me, and tears welled up in her eyes when she saw the unmistakable resolve on my face. It was a look of fixed obedience that said I was going to do exactly what I had been told to do.

It was next to impossible to find the Carlsons on any given Sunday at O.F.E., as we had so deftly rearranged our schedules not to have to see each other. I confidently walked into the Educational Christianity building, resting in the knowledge that a divine encounter was imminent. No sooner had I turned a corner than I walked straight into Lorne and Candice Carlson! Something was telltale in my face as I beamed forgiveness even with my invitation: "Please—I need to talk to both of you as soon as it is possible."

It was no surprise to me that God had cleared everyone's calendars so that we could meet directly that Sunday night at our house on Chestnut Street. When we had settled into our living room, I came right to the point: "Lorne, Candice, I need to ask you to forgive me for what I put you both through two years ago. I accept full responsibility for the mess we were in. I know now that, whatever you did was out of desperation and survival—a situation of my own making. If you can't forgive me, I will completely understand. I know that I have scarred you. I am sorry. Again, please forgive me for all that I put you through."

No sooner had I paused than Candice leapt up from her chair, with tears in her eyes. "Of course, we forgive you, Ian!" She hugged me so hard it took my breath away. We cried. Maria hugged Lorne, and they, too, cried. Then we switched until every combination of the foursome had hugged and cried. We then became aware of a brand-new sensation about the room—a manifest lightness in the very air. All rancor, acrimony, bitterness, scars, and hurt had been completely removed from our presence, in an instant! I felt akin to lighter-than-air Puritan Hester Prynne from Nathaniel Hawthorne's *The Scarlet Letter* when she explained that she did not understand the full extent of her burden until she had tasted freedom.

We were eyewitnesses to a Divine wall-breaking ceremony. Immediate. Miraculous. Complete. And wonderfully irreparable. I recalled the lesson from Joshua I had taught so many years before to not ever try to rebuild what God had so miraculously torn down. We would also heed that warning! We intended to fully enjoy and cherish forever what God had given back to us, and to let anyone who cared to know just exactly *Who* was responsible for our reconciliation and restoration. This may not happen all the time to everyone in this way. All we know is that it happened to us!

Sometimes Christians can get themselves all worked up into a smug, self-righteous, torch-bearing witch-hunt, combing the forest for that horned guy in the red suit carrying a pitchfork. I think that Satan has tossed many a rock into distant bushes in order to make rustling decoys. The frothing mob is thrown off track so easily by being diverted to the sounds of the obvious. They pounce on the bush and set fire to it with their torches. Divergent bushes—better known as Halloween, movies, television, music—can all have certain elements of devilish descent. But as the smoke gets in their eyes, Satan scampers to the *other* side of the forest and ravages our churches, our marriages, our children, and our friendships.

Some weeks after God had resurrected our friendship with the Carlsons, I found myself rummaging through the desk in our office-bedroom upstairs. In an effort not to give that parasite Satan anymore footholds, I thoroughly searched through every drawer and cubby-hole until I found what I was looking for. I made a couple of phone calls to some fellow members of the Deacon Board, walked down the stairs, out the front door, and down to the corner of our block.

I mailed my letter to Sheldon Abbott.

When I had finished the end of my four-year term on the Deacon Board at Our Father's Evangelical Church, I decided to return an eternal favor. I stepped down from the Board—not opting for a second term—and quit all other adult teaching responsibilities. With the cessation of all my previous ministries, I became a Sunday school teacher for the boys in the 5th-grade Department.

I exchanged all the mini-pulpits throughout the church for a metal folding chair in a 10 x 12 room in the Educational Christianity building. I had the satisfying sense of completing an important circle for me as I opened the 5th-grade curriculum and did my best at making the next hour a three-dimensional biblical thrill ride through all of the twists, turns, loops, drops, dips and "G" forces found in the pages of Scripture for Sean, Leonard, Alex, and Robert—a new generation of Four Musketeers!

We made a deal early on in our acquaintance that, if I ever got too pumped-up and preachy, my new 5th-graders were to call me on the forest-green carpet by saying the one sentence that would stop me in my tracks: "Mr. Block, pick on someone your own size!"

To which I would respond,

"Uh, sorry, kids—my mirror got a little foggy!"

CHAPTER EIGHT

SAYING HIS PRAYERS.

"Taste and see that the Lord is good." A young David (after recently feigning mental insanity in order to save his own skin) yells this very sane dare into a tin can which is connected by more than 1,000 years of string to another tin can in the future. Holding this tin can to his ear on the other side of the millennia canyon is Saint Peter, who, after hearing David's words, reminds his correspondents that they, too, "have tasted that the Lord is good."

I am not so sure that I feel the goodness of the Lord right now, as I have spent most of my day at Our Father's Evangelical Church—not in the role of ex-deacon or Bible teacher but in the role of Insurance Agent, as a fire broke out in the church kitchen last night during the annual "Canes and Able" Seniors' Banquet.

It started with some very hot grease and was fanned into quite the conflagration that caused the evacuation of our gymnasium and the burning out of most of the church kitchen. The Monument Fire Department was heroic in their assistance in not only dousing the fire with gallons of water, but also in offering care and concern for the Seniors, whose frazzled emotions were slightly charred as well.

I received a fretful call from Frank Petry, the appointed leader for the Seniors at O.F.E., and I immediately sped over to the church. The Monument Fire Department had already arrived, and all of the forlorn Seniors were gathered on the front lawn of the church. After plowing my way through the throngs of spectators that had formed around the church property, I spent most of that night and the next morning haggling with Claims Adjusters and Beulah Argyle, who was the short and stout, self-appointed Joan of Arc of the O.F.E. kitchen. She had assumed the coveted culinary role shortly after my Grandmother Frances passed away. Grandma Frances had been a talented cafeteria lady for the Monument School District during her career, and, so, after her retirement, she ran our church kitchen with extreme efficiency. When she died, Beulah Argyle, who had been salivating at the job for years, leapt right into the Frances void, putting on the hairnet and plastic gloves before anyone else had a chance to be considered for the position.

With the kitchen her supreme domain, it was necessary for me to listen to Beulah tell her dramatic version of the fire and nod my head as she berated not only the archaic refrigerators, stoves, pots, and pans, but also the hazards of improperly used grease. "How anyone could expect me to cook for several hundred people at one time in this kitchen is beyond me!"

And yet she would crank out meal after meal for social after social, wielding her military might over the utensils and appliances, forcing them into palatable submission.

When Beulah had finished her testimony (and tirade!), I walked around the gymnasium area, where the fire had wrought the most damage. Some areas were still smoking, floors were flooded, and the exterior walls were blackened.

It was going to be a long, complicated, difficult loss to service, and it was only the beginning! Understandably, I came home the next afternoon exhausted, smelling of smoke, with black streaks all over my face. I looked like the overcooked main course from the "Canes and Able" Banquet, and felt like it!

This would have been so much easier had my father been able to assist me. But he was "indisposed" at the moment and could only offer cursory advice by long-distance over the phone, as he and my mother had sold their house on Vista Street and had moved up north! I remember how shocked Owen and I were when we heard the news. My mother and father had invited all of the family over for what we thought was just an informal dinner. After dessert, my father broke the news to us.

Owen was still coaching in Los Angeles. He had married my sister-in-law, Penny, a few years before. They now had a baby boy, Owen, Jr. Along with our two daughters, we made for a full house on Vista Street that night when my father sprung the news of their migration.

I asked my always stick-it-out-to-the-bitter-end father how he came up with this idea. His response to me was, "The house is too big for us to maintain, and we no longer need all of this room." He was still going to retain ownership of Block Insurance but would hand over the managing duties to me and our small staff. They tried to pacify us by informing us that they had

". . . bought into a beautiful retirement community right by the ocean. We are not going to be too far away; we can still drive down here anytime!"

I guess what bothered Owen and me most of all was the selling off of all the poignant memories of our home: the Christmases, birthday parties, and graduations. Now complete strangers would live within the walls of our pasts. In spite of its size, I prayed I would never sell our house on Chestnut Street and pull the memory rug out from underneath my children. I was happy that my parents were simplifying their lives, but, always the Insurance Agent, I smelled the smoke from the bridge burning behind me.

Over the next few weeks, I came to realize that most of the job of simplifying my parents' lives had actually fallen upon Owen and me, as we helped clean out the house on Vista Street and noticed from the outset that my parents had not thrown *anything* away! We went through as many boxes as was possible and did our best to divvy up the spoils between either Owen and me when we felt any sentimental attachment toward a particular possession.

Given the constraints of time conveniently provided for by the pending closing of escrow, I had to take home carloads of antiquities no longer necessary for my parents. When I carried the artifacts into our house, their dubious, *current* necessity was viciously questioned by Maria! To keep peace in my own family, I carted up all the Vista Street entrails to our spare office-bedroom. "Out of sight, out of mind," was my conclusion as I shut the office-bedroom door after stacking the boxes up against the room's walls, creating a singular path through a brown-cardboard canyon to the desk in the corner.

"Someday, when I get a chance, I will go through all that stuff."

Since Maria used our new computer at the desk occasionally, she had some trouble concentrating while interned in a claustrophobic cardboard prison. The purging of the office-bedroom never left her "to do" list!

Months after my parents were comfortably settled into their new condo up north, and at the consistent behest of Maria, I cracked one Saturday when my excuses had run dry, and I walked up the stairs to that dreadful room in which lurked the stockpile of boxes that had somehow escaped the capital punishment of a garage sale.

I opened boxes for hours on end: toys, broken clock radios, records, record players, comic books, recipe boxes, old lamps, a fishing tackle box. Most of the proceeds from my labors ended up in the trash cans outside. Occasionally, I would find something of value and would try to integrate it (with or without Maria's knowledge) into the menagerie of things that were already in our house!

After lunch, dinner, and my daughters' bedtimes, I still had not made a significant dent and continued to "pry open the past" until late into the evening. Even after Maria had gone on to bed, I became obsessed with seeing this project through and even enjoyed some of the reminiscences the exercise was providing.

While sitting on the office-bedroom floor, I opened one box that had a folded, bulky, faded, wine-colored silky comforter I remembered from my Grandmother Melba. "This box must have been overlooked by my parents. I am sure they would not have parted with this," I said to myself. The oversight must have been due to the rushed packing that characterized my parents' move. Then I realized that this particular box must have been one of the many my parents had acquired when *they* had cleaned out my *grandparents'* home in preparation for its sale after their deaths. This box was probably left over from my own father's procrastination in going through *his* father's acquisitions. My mother had apparently not prodded him long enough!

Below the folded comforter was a smaller box, or chest, as it were. It had those old metal protective edges and corners, and the faded blue corduroy cloth that lined it was tattered and torn. I snapped up the silver clasp and opened the lid. Strewn all over the top of the chest were a variety of old, bent black-and-white photos. Some were of people I had never seen before; some of the backgrounds were of Monument, but the buildings I was familiar with now either looked completely different or had ceased to exist altogether. There were some brown-tinted-with-age photos that even showed our mountainside *without* the Rudolph Valentino carving! My Grandmother Melba was in some, looking younger than Maria! In another, Colby Block was standing at attention in his World War I Army uniform, his feet firmly planted on the front lawn of a residence that was completely isolated by acreage from any other houses and commercial buildings that now crowded out the very same plot of land. Apparently, he was just leaving, or on leave, or something. The uniform in the picture is actually now on display in the Monument Museum, down by the freeway. Our family has toured the museum many times. The uniform is worn by one of the many mannequins in a gripping World War I display. My father donated the uniform to the museum not only due to its authenticity (as my grandfather had actually fought in that war) but also because Colby Block had been one of the oldest living natives of our town before he died.

I peeled off layers of photos and carefully laid them on the floor. A more detailed perusal would come later. Underneath was an old book with a thick brown cardboard binding. I took it out of the box and delicately opened it. On the front page was written, in what was once very bold lettering (now significantly faded) the words, *"Mental Blocks."* Below the title, under the word "by," was what appeared to be my grandfather's signature.

After a few turns of the yellowed pages, I realized that I was reading a journal of my grandfather's! I shut the book and moved to the desk chair. I turned on the desk lamp. The rest of the unpacking would have to wait. My curiosity at this strange discovery superseded any sense of duty at finishing my formidable, daylong task.

My grandfather had never mentioned such a book. Neither had my grandmother, nor my father. It must have been kept a secret. I felt like I was in some "B" movie! The well-worn plot device of finding someone's secret diary was so predictable and downright campy. I was embarrassed at the similarities, and yet here I was, sitting on the desk chair, surrounded by the cluttered floor of our office-bedroom, the only one awake in the house, under the yellowish oval provided by the singular lamp from the desk, with the journal of my taciturn grandfather, Colby Block, sitting on my lap! Any minute now, the studio house lights would come on, and a director would yell "Cut! Print!" Or maybe I would just wake up from this silly dream!

"Well, truth is stranger than fiction," I said to myself out loud to make sure that I was, in fact, awake. I opened the book once again.

"Mental Blocks—Prayers and Observations by Colby Block." was written on the second page, along with a date, *"September 30, 1912."* The book was filled with pithy entries describing events in the life of Colby Block. I guess he meant them to be prayers as they all started with the word, "Lord." Interspersed between these personal entries were excerpts from the actual book of Psalms. They were culled from a lineup of the most

famous psalter passages from that ancient hymnal, such as 23, 51, and 91. These must have been copied directly from Colby Block's own Bible, which was then in my parents' possession, ornamenting a coffee table in a condo at a beach community to the north of Monument.

I turned a couple of the fragile pages and read,

"October 10, 1912: Lord, thanks for allowing me to go out with Doris Wallace last night. I can't believe she's even interested in me. Help me to have the guts to ask her to go steady. I like her very much, Lord."

I wondered if my grandfather was possibly speaking of his high-school sweetheart, Doris Mackintosh! This was impossible for me to confirm, as I did not know her maiden name. There was, however, an old sepia photo tucked within the pages depicting a high-school-aged girl, but I could not recognize any of her youthful features.

He went on for the next few pages to describe the trials and tribulations of dating this new heartthrob of his. From what I could read through the barely legible writing, faded words, smudges, and tears, it had been a short-lived romance that was fun while it lasted.

The book was also cluttered with clippings and various and sundry papers and pictures that were all sticking out at haphazard angles, making the dilapidated volume appear like a potential scrapbook with all of the to-be-added items carelessly jammed into its pages, awaiting a more methodical placement in some distant future.

As I continued to turn the pages, a flaking, folded newspaper clipping fell into my lap. It was in French and apparently from some Parisian newspaper which was dated August 3, 1915. The entry on the page was of the same date:

"August 3, 1915: Lord, Lieutenant Lewis is really putting the pressure on me as he has frowned on my religion since I enlisted. Please help Miller, Swanson, and me to keep up the faith. It is getting harder every day to serve you in war."

It was eerie to picture my 20-year-old grandfather marching around Paris, France, during World War I, wearing a uniform that his great-grandchildren had seen many times at the Monument Museum, 63 years before Maria and I would become engaged in that very same city!

Towards the center of the prayer journal was a small square cutout from a *Webster's Dictionary*. It was no surprise to see the word that had been excerpted included among the other scraps in the journal,

"Sycophant: informer, swindler, sycophant; a servile, self-seeking flatterer."
(I could have used this definition years ago!)

It was getting very late into the night when I turned to a page about two-thirds into the journal, whose first words stopped me cold. It was dated May 13, 1933.

"Lord, please forgive me, but I need to leave this church. I am sorry if this disappoints you, but I cannot see any other way out of this. Please do not think of me as a prodigal. I will not leave you. I know my sweet Melba will be faithful to the church. I just cannot. She is sad, and so am I.

I know you are working hard to make the church great, but I cannot wait around for you to make it healthy. I think I can be of better use to you on the outside. I'm sorry, Lord. This is probably a mistake I'll regret. But I am determined. I won't forget you."

Folded into this page were a couple of aged sheets of note-book paper from 1933. As I unfolded them with all the gentle dexterity I could muster, a foreboding feeling swelled inside of me and made my stomach's butterflies take chaotic flight.

By the time I had spread the papers onto the desk, I was fully prepared for what I was about to see, as the seconds of anticipation had caused me to expect this. The furrowed notebook-paper samples had obviously been torn from some larger book, as the left-hand sides had been carelessly ripped from top to bottom. These were an original transcription of a deacon meeting at Our Father's Evangelical Church dated May 12, 1933. As I expected, these were not the minutes from just *any* deacon meeting—they were, apparently, the minutes from *the* deacon meeting.

I looked up from the papers. Any moment now, a director was going to yell for the script writer to rework this scene! It was implausible and predictable. Or was it? I could not concern myself with the believability of my situation at the moment. I was more interested in the believability of what I was about to read.

Written in longhand (in a style that was definitely not my grand-father's), was the following:

To: Members of the Deacon Board From: Noel Saunders, Secretary
Subject: Deacon Board Meeting Minutes from May 12, 1933

Saying His Prayers.

Present: Wyatt Dupont, Farley Dobbs, Earl Swietzer, Charles Pendleton, Colby Block, Morgan Pierce, Roy Mueller, Franklin Mullens, and myself.

Unable to Attend: None

1. *After opening in prayer, the meeting was called to order by Chairman Dupont.*

2. *Monthly budget was approved.*

3. *Morgan Pierce discussed needed repairs for the main sanctuary.*

4. *Charlie Pendleton gave an update on Bartholomew and Lydia Pratt, and their missionary call to the Philippines.*

5. *Chairman Dupont asked for an update on the special meeting last month calling our new Senior Pastor, Wesley Zimmerman, to the church. The congregational call was an 81% "yea" vote, with only 35% of the membership reporting. The Board was concerned about the representation of the congregation, but had agreed to call Pastor Zimmerman to the church.*

6. *Colby Block expressed his concerns about the voting tally. He also raised the issue of housing for the new pastor and his family. They were to arrive during the next week, and Pastor Zimmerman would officially report to work on May 18.*

I carefully turned over the page.

7. *Further discussion regarding the representation in the voting tally:*

Roy Mueller asked for permission to leave the room. He returned with a box. He then stated to the Board that this box was found in the trunk of Morgan Pierce's vehicle earlier that week. The box was handed to Chairman Dupont, who opened it. The box contained hundreds of completed church voting ballots from the congregational meeting a month prior.

Chairman Dupont asked Morgan Pierce to explain the box of ballots found in his vehicle.

8. *Morgan Pierce confessed he was serious about Wesley Zimmerman being called to the church. He knew in his heart he was God's man for the job. He did not trust the congregation to make a mature decision, so he had confiscated all of the ballots that were against Pastor Zimmerman.*

9. *Farley Dobbs, Treasurer, had taken ill on the night of the meeting, so Morgan Pierce had volunteered to take his place in the task of counting ballots. He stated he came up with the idea as he was counting the ballots.*

10. *Colby Block stated his objections at any member of the Deacon Board counting money or ballots alone. It was stated by Chairman Dupont that "this was highly irregular and is not our normal procedure, as Farley Dobbs always had companions to witness and verify any of his actions."*

The writing on the letter grew more and more rushed and urgent. The business-like handwriting of these minutes was gradually forfeited and gave way to a more frantic scrawl in just trying to keep up. Whoever Noel Saunders was, it looked like he had abandoned his official Secretarial position and now had became a Sports Reporter, calling the shots in real time of the rapid-fire events from increasingly petulant Board members, that would have to be edited and transcribed more legibly later.

I turned to the next page.

11. *Farley Dobbs yelled at Morgan Pierce, "You rigged the election! Zimmerman should not be coming here at all!" Morgan Pierce responded, "Yes he should, Farley—it just goes to show how much you know about leadership in the church!"*

Wyatt Dupont tried to interrupt, but Farley and Morgan were far too loud by this time. Wyatt tried again to yell over them and have them apologize for the salty language they were using. Morgan Pierce stood up at the same time as Farley Dobbs. Farley walked over and hit Morgan Pierce in the face, knocking him to the floor. Colby Block came over and separated the two men after they had locked into a fierce fistfight.

Someone yelled, "The vote is void!" And someone else yelled back, "It's too late, he's already coming!" I also heard "The damage is done!" "God help us!" "God help you, Pierce!" Afterwards, Wyatt makes everyone sit down to cool off. He says we will make the best of the situation by standing behind Pastor Zimmerman. Colby Block stands up and asks the Chairman to speak a few words. Chairman Dupont grants Colby some time,

"I have never b

The bottom left-hand corner of the second page had been torn off at this point—the apparent result of the sudden extraction of the papers from the original notebook? Consequently, there was no further distinguishable writing.

I sat back in the desk chair and sighed. It was extraordinary. For however long Pastor Zimmerman had lasted, the Deacon Board had apparently made a united front behind a newly called Senior Pastor who had not been called at all! Since there was already an official minutes to this meeting of May 12, 1933, submitted and recorded in the church archives (I verified this as soon as I was placed on the Deacon Board), it is evident that the board must have decided to cover up the actual events of the debacle in order to save face. My grandfather probably could not abide by this and had stormed out of the meeting.

He must have battled with his own conscience in not blowing the whistle on his fellow board members. Maybe it was his word being his bond or something like that. Or, perhaps he'd struck a deal with them and obtained the only copy of the actual minutes as collateral in hasty exchange for their silence in never including his name in public discourses pertaining to the Deacon Board meeting.

I could never even check on the veracity of the contents of these papers, as the people who might corroborate this story even by hearsay were long since dead. The likes of Cyril Holbert, Virgil Cronklin, or even Walter Mackintosh might have been helpful but, regretfully, I had fallen prey to that old pirate slogan, "Dead men tell no tales!" What with the migratory habits of Southern Californians these days, most of the friends and families of those early O.F.E. members have either moved away or died off themselves.

Perhaps they knew nothing further about the events, anyway.

So I folded up the papers and placed them back into Colby Block's prayer book. It was too much information to digest in one sitting. I would return to these mysteries later and try to sort it all out. In the meantime, I decided I would keep this discovery between Maria and myself. Someday soon, I would ask my father if he could substantiate any of this. It now appears that the original rumors about the deacon- meeting details with my grandfather that I had heard over the years were all wrong. I would not heap additional inflammatory fuel speculating on what was already error.

I skimmed toward the end of the book to the last entry, dated June 15, 1979. My grandfather was even secretly writing in his journal during my lifetime!

For whatever reason, this was his last entry:

"Lord, please be with Ian as he goes up to camp. Please show him who you are in a whole new way. He's a great kid and I love him. Bring him back to us safely. I am also getting concerned about Melba's forgetfulness. It seems to be getting worse. I have the feeling she's getting senile. Please Lord, I want her to go home to you first so that she can be spared the pain of being left behind. I want to take on her loss myself. Please Lord, if her condition is a sign then please take her when it is time and spare her from being the one who is left of the two of us. Thank you for her and our life together. In spite of my behavior, Lord, you have really blessed me."

Perhaps the mounting care for my grandmother had encroached upon his writing efforts.

Regardless, even with his flaws, my grandfather's prayer for me was answered two days later on a hilltop at the Cheyenne Christian Conference Center.

Less than a year later, God answered my grandfather's second final recorded prayer.

I closed the book, *for now.* I shoved it far back into a desk drawer and went, very much preoccupied, on to bed.

Weeks after my discovery in our office-bedroom (even though I was much older than my grandfather had been), I was convicted to start my own prayer journal. I went to the store and purchased a very thick, blank-paged diary in anticipation of the reams of spiritual nuggets and gems I would place into it. The color was light blue and a little too cutesy for me, but it was all I could find at the time that would suffice.

That evening, I sat at the still-cardboard-box-cluttered-office-bedroom desk and opened my journal to the first page. Since my primary inspiration for starting my own prayer journal was Colby Block, and I was merely being a steward of his secretive example, I called my prayer journal

"Mental Ward—Prayers and Observations by Ian Block."

I also wrote below my name a Psalm slice my grandfather had included in his journal:

"One generation will commend your works to another."

I turned the page and taped my first entry into the book. It was cut from my own *Webster's Dictionary:*

"Synopsis: A seeing, visual image: A statement giving a brief, general review or condensation, summary."

The balance of the book remained blank for many days afterwards. I could not think of a fitting entry to start my journal. Unlike David, Solomon, Asaph, and Korah, I was not a gifted lyricist of all things heavenly. Then, one evening while I was driving home from work, a song came on my Honda's car radio that was instantly qualified to be my journal's Grand Marshall, proudly marching before my potential parade of future sagacious thoughts:

A little boy sitting on a metal folding chair,
in what appears to be a Sunday school room.
He could see that shepherd boy, his sling up in the air,
he could feel that giant hit with a boom.

In that room I saw the Red Sea part,
and two by two animals get in the ark.
And Mrs. Keen gently would say,
The God of the past is still God today.

So tell me again of the old, old stories.
Tell me again of the faithful who walked,
in the lion's den and the fiery furnace,
of Noah and rainbows and donkeys that talked.
I don't want to forget so please, tell me again.

A young man sitting at a desk with a wooden chair,
In what appears to be a high school class.
He can see a battlefield there's giants everywhere saying,
"The Bible is a thing of the past."
In this new age you believe what you want to believe,
'Cause god is whatever you want it to be,
and I can hear Mrs. Keen gently say,
The God of the past is still God today.

So tell me again of the old, old stories.
Tell me again of the faithful who walked,
in the lion's den and the fiery furnace,
of Noah and rainbows and donkeys that talked.
I don't want to forget so please, tell me again.

How the God of the ages,
turned history's pages and saw my need.
Tell me again of the shepherds and wise men,
and the star that would lead them to the baby who was born,
so that we could be born again.

Tell me again of the Gospel story.
Tell me again how the whole world was lost.
How the Only Begotten with grace so amazing,
gave up His life on an old rugged cross.
I don't want to forget so please, tell me again.

Tell me again of the old, old stories.
Tell me again of the faithful who walked.
How the Only Begotten, with grace so amazing,
gave up His life on an old rugged cross.

I don't want to forget so please, tell me again.

My 39th year had been a very busy one! First, we reconciled
with the Carlsons, and then my parents moved up north, followed by the O.F.E. kitchen fire, and lastly, the discovery of my
grandfather's secret prayer journal! By the end of the summer,
it was time for a much-needed vacation!

In the spirit of those eventful road trips from my past, our family decided to drive up north and see the natural wonders of the Sierra Nevadas. It was also agreed that one of our stopovers would be the Cheyenne Christian Conference Center. It had been 18 years since I had been on staff, and I was drawn to the idea of returning.

Upon our arrival, we settled in at the Pine Tree Lodge, a quaint, comfortable motel for family travelers to the camp, complete with all the modern conveniences and tasteful rustic-themed accoutrements. It was a far cry from the oppressive Boot Hill, which was still perched on its lonely hill, 18 years further advanced in the school of disrepair.

As I had not set foot in the camp since my Accommodations Staff days, the Cheyenne Christian Conference Center seemed a perfectly preserved time capsule. This caused me to be bombarded with memories. It felt like the hordes of disturbed gnats that surround your head when you have hiked too near a secluded, stagnant eddy of a lake and disrupted the bugs' skimming of the steamy surface and their darting around the grass-infested shallows.

Everywhere we turned, I saw the ghosts of fellow staff members and could vividly recall some occasion or antic. My family indulged me during the days we spent at the camp—hiking, boating, and swimming—as I was a constant verbal stream of stories from the Summer of 1979.

One night, as we were sitting on the dock of the lake, looking up at the garish firmament strewn with brilliant stars and waiting to catch a possible glimpse of that all-too-brief, elusive shooting star, our family conversation turned toward my first few hours after arriving at the camp, and my little "chat" with

God. Sharayah and Samantha were riveted to this story, more so than other memory lanes I had dragged them down thus far. Still, with great emotional difficulty, I finished the testimony of my first "theophany." They then asked if I would take them to the sacred hilltop the next day. I agreed.

The hillside looked much different than it had before. So many seasons of snow, rain, frost, and heat combinations had rearranged the topography significantly. But I found the deteriorating fallen log still lying in its original and final resting place. The four of us sat down on the log together. We were silent for quite some time as the air seemed thick with the residue of my story from the night before. I finally felt compelled to break the silence and said softly, while staring reverently at the pine-needled ground, tears beginning to form in my eyes,

"Girls, if you ever face a time in your lives when you doubt the existence of God, or you think He doesn't care, even long after I am dead and gone, walk up this hill. In whatever feeble way I have tried to introduce Him to you, it all became clear to me right here."

This last line nudged Sharayah's inquisitiveness. "Dad, what do you mean 'it all became clear to you'? Didn't you become a Christian when you were, like, eight years old?"

"Yes, I did. I am talking about a clear *understanding* that what my parents—your grandparents—believed is now true for me as well!"

"What do you mean?" To my great satisfaction, Sharayah wanted to get to the bottom of this.

"Let me put it to you this way, Honey. After I had been up here at camp for more than half of the summer, your Grandpa Seth and Grandma Nancy came up for a visit. I had not seen them in over six weeks. I had left them in Monument for the very first time as a 21-year-old struggling with who he was and where he was going."

I turned my head around and pointed up through a pass in the tall grove of pine trees. "I was working far up that canyon back there, mopping the 'Panting Deer Eatin' Hall' of the 'Twelve Tribes' Junior Camp. Another Accommodations truck pulled up to tell me that my parents had arrived. I quickly left my crew to finish the floors and jumped into my own Accommodations truck and sped down that windy dirt road over there to the main parking lot down by the lake. I jumped out of the truck and could instantly see the back of my mother, who was standing at the opposite end of the parking lot, staring out at the beautiful lake. Your Grandfather Seth must have been in the Camp Administration Office, either checking on their reservations or my whereabouts. He did not know that I had been tipped off to their arrival!

"Anyway, I walked up to your grandmother, the large ring of keys jingling at my side alerting her that someone was coming. She turned around and saw me." I smiled at the recollection. "I must have been quite a sight! My Cheyenne Christian Conference Center navy-blue staff shirt, a red bandana tied around my neck, a hammer hanging from my painter's pants, big, brown-stained, tan plumber's boots, all topped off by that official ring of important-looking keys! But what must have changed the most was the look on my face. I could feel myself giving it. I could not help myself! As we were briskly walking toward each other, she must have seen the look in my eyes, and we embraced. It was one of the tightest, most celebratory Mama Bear hugs I had ever received from her. I hugged her right back just as tightly, saying with my whole body, 'I get it, Mother! I, too, have now met the Heavenly Father intimately, and I get it now. Your faith has become mine!'"

Sharayah, Samantha, and Maria stared at me while I fought back and choked down a flood of reminiscent tears. "You know," I continued through the emotional congestion, "we weren't a very affectionate family. So a hug like that from your Grandmother Nancy was powerful and meaningful. A moment like that has happened only twice."

"When was the other time, Dad?" Sharayah asked.

"When I walked into the waiting room of the Monument Hospital to announce to your four grandparents that your mother had given birth to *you*, Sharayah! For some reason, I gravitated to your Grandma Nancy and hugged her first. That same, knowing tight clench that said to an older parent from a brand-new one, 'I get it now! The indescribable feeling of seeing your newborn baby for the very first time!'"

Sharayah stood up from the log. "Oh, I think I get it now."

"So do I, Daddy!" Samantha chimed in, wanting to contribute to the conversation and hopping up from the log as well.

"I will always pray that you do," I said as Maria stood up last and gave me her own version of a Mama Bear hug.

After a few moments of silently watching their parents embrace, and, hopefully weighing my previous words, Sharayah, Samantha, and then Maria started to slowly hike back down the hillside. I lingered for one last private moment, not knowing when or if I would ever return to this meaningful spot.

I stood up and looked back down at the fallen log and pictured that 21-year-old boy with his face in his hands, sobbing. That boy was me! I choked out a prayer, "Oh, God, after all we have been through together, I want so badly to tell that boy it is going to be okay."

I wanted to drop the tin can from my mouth, run back in time across 18 years of string, give that 21-year-old boy a Papa Bear hug, and lovingly whisper into his ear,

"Son, I have tasted that the Lord is good!"

EPILOGUE

"a little folding of the hands to rest—"

—Proverbs 6:10b

BANG!

The explosion of the 14th helium balloon jarred me from my pen-and-paper stalemate. I took off my glasses (yes, glasses!) and rubbed my tired eyes and the bridge of my nose. I got up from the couch and walked around our living room. At least half of the helium balloons were losing their battle with gravity and were helplessly descending to the living-room floor. The colorful streamers were still draped in twisted, serpentine celebration around the circumference of the room. There were even some plastic cups and crumpled napkins still littering the available surfaces of the coffee table, end tables, and erected T.V. trays. The party had ended so late into the evening that Maria and I had only marginally cleaned up afterwards. The balance of putting the house back in order lay in wait for us tomorrow morning. Now I was the only one who remained awake among the occupants of our home. The others were currently sleeping off the recent soiree that had been given in my honor.

I halted my pacing at the oval mirror that was adjacent to our fireplace mantle and peeked in at the intruder. For some reason, I was gripped with a twinge of disbelief at the veracity of the reflection and pushed my face intrusively into the psychological space of the face looking back at me. Aside from the tributaries of wrinkles that were distinguishing my face with ever-increasing complexity, there were also widening swaths of gray streaking my thinning, dishwater-blond hair. I craned my neck to look downwards into the reflection to see if there might be more encouragement in the unseen portion below the median of the beveled bottom edge of the mirror. To my dismay, the passage of time had also been sufficiently deleterious to those portions below the waistline. Bulging contours were providing visual detours to my previously svelte frame. *Face it, Ian—you're not as lanky as you used to be! Maybe not even as tall, either!* My "fearfully and wonderfully made" womb-formed earthly shell was deteriorating and joining together in a rousing chorus of "Happy Birthday to You!"

As of today, I am now 40. The party Maria and the kids had thrown was a smashing success. Our living room was filled with family, friends, and acquaintances representing every stage of my life. Maria had even tracked down Nathan Raab and Kenneth Ball, who flew in for the occasion (no one knew the whereabouts of Patrick Hamilton). My mother and father, Paulo and Nicole, Owen, Penny, Owen, Jr. (who was screaming most of the time), and Malcolm Davis were in attendance, just to name a few! Even Milton and Amber Derringer made a cameo appearance, but he had to cut out early as more sermon preparation was necessary for the upcoming Sunday services.

Maria had outdone herself with the sumptuous food (Italian, of course!), some hilarious games, and then the awkward and embarrassing testimonials from the invitees as they would relate their own, hilarious at times, versions of the fancies and *faux pas* of Ian Block. I was cajoled into making a brief speech at the end of the "roast." I thanked my family and friends for making this special evening happen and for the wide array of gag gifts that had been so thoughtfully presented! I ended my little appreciative retrospect with a spontaneous line that oozed more profundity than intended: "In closing, here's to 40 years of the abundant life, 'cause that's exactly what it's been!"

I used to think my eight-year-old childhood conversion to Christianity was such a yawner compared to the sensational, successful rescues from sex, drugs, and Rock 'n Roll of so many of my fellow saints around me. My self-consciousness was ratified one Thanksgiving Eve service in our main sanctuary when Sheldon Abbott had asked the O.F.E. members to voluntarily walk up to any one of a number of strategically placed microphones and state for what they were most thankful. When it was Peter Grant's turn, he confidently walked up to the microphone closest to his seat and succinctly said, "I am thankful that I have no testimony."

This drew a smattering of "Amens" from the crowd. They knew exactly what he meant! Thankfully (or regretfully?), so did I!

I came to realize later that whether it was a pricked finger's drop of blood wedged between two rectangular glass platelets examined under a microscope, or a profusely bleeding, gushing flesh wound spilling all over the place, God bleeding for anyone, to any degree, is globally newsworthy!

So, whether it took a dropper or a gallon of blood to save the soul of Ian Block, or whether it would take a pint or quart of blood to keep him sanctified, it was enough to stop the heartbeat of God's human form. And the same otherworldly power that plunged down and re-activated that heart three days later re-activated mine at eight years old. Now *that*, too, is globally newsworthy!

> *"It streams from the hills, it descends to the plain,*
> *and sweetly distills in the dew and the rain."*

After the last of our guests had left the house (which, of course, were Lorne and Candice Carlson!), my little party speech had motivated me to write my reflections in another installment of *"Mental Ward—Prayers and Observations by Ian Block."* The journal was progressing at a snail's pace, but it was at least (imperceptibly?) moving forward. I had even included a selection of my silly Bible character cartoons to add some variety to what I deemed was rather banal and insipid prose. After all, who would read this, anyway? An as-yet-nonexistent grandchild or great-grandchild going through the frustrating exercise of sifting through accumulated clutter and debatable valuables and discovering an all-too-feminine-looking light-blue journal filled with the pithy epistles and love notes to God from some pack-rat predecessor?

I sat back down on the couch and picked up my journal again. Now it was *very* late into the night! It might have been the infant hours of the next day as far as I knew—I did not bother to check. I wanted to record the details of my 40th birthday before any middle-aged cobwebs formed around the powers of my recall. I stared at the last recorded sentence fragment long enough for it to blur and for any new inspirational musings to be locked out. I put down the pen and rubbed my hands, giving them an undeserved rest. I seem to have inherited my mother's arthritic-finger infestation. While I was massaging my fingers, I endeavored to conjure up some philosophical brilliance about my half-finished life.

The *obvious* symbolism was carved up the hillside a couple of miles from our house, right behind Our Father's Evangelical Church (with its newly repaired kitchen and gymnasium). Only it was not so obvious anymore. This last winter had drenched us with such an overabundance of rainfall that it caused the mountains behind Monument to be embellished with lush, aggressive bushes and shrubbery growing at beanstalk speed to encompass the mountainside in a full five o'clock shadow of ever-expanding foliage. As a result, the cracked, noseless, earless half-face of Rudolph Valentino was almost completely obscured. Until recently, the City would hire workers to trim back the invading growth in order to keep the tourist attraction attractive. But the years of erosion and shifts in the Pacific plates over the past 50 years have caused the movie star to crack and peel in such a way that he was rapidly becoming an anticlimax at first sight. The City officials finally decided to let nature run its stubborn course and gradually cover our now-disappointing City's namesake.

Nevertheless, Rudolph was still up there, somewhere, the aging half-head providing ample movie-script symbolism for my reflections on my middle-aged life. Now, I could spiritualize my "monumental" age with the biblical metaphor of the Potter and the half-finished jar of clay: Can I truly say with confidence to the Potter, "Go ahead and pump the pedal and spin the wheel! *Mold me and make me after Thy will*"?

Or, maybe a *Michelangelo* analogy would be fitting: I am a 40-year-old, half-finished block of marble, and the famous sculptor is in the process of chipping out a biblical classic. Can I truly say, "Go ahead, hack away, Michel—just watch the arms!"?

Or, perhaps I could say of all three Rudolph representations that the movie idols of this world, the false gods, and all of our best artistic efforts and creative feats are eventually going to fade away in the *"light of His glory and grace."*

Also, am I really excited about what lies ahead? I know there are watershed moments of joy in the future: graduations of my daughters from high school and, hopefully, college (could I interest them in an application to the Antioch Christian Academy?), keeping my composure and giving them away at their weddings, that first grandchild. But I'm sure there are also an equal number of counter-acting tragedies ahead as well. That's just life in a fallen world, as they say. So, will getting there really be *half* the fun?

Truth be told, Maria and I are terrified, with our daughters standing on the brink of those dreaded teenage years that are right around the corner for Sharayah, and, in the blink of an eye, for Samantha as well! It is not only the "who" they are growing up to be that preoccupies us, but also the "what," "where," and "when" of the light and dark influences. Properly raising godly teenage daughters in Southern California at the end of the 1990s seems a bit like sweeping the ocean! Sometimes Maria and I mentally entertain that escape hatch that is probably more cop-out than awe-inspired excitement for Thy Kingdom Coming: How about a nice Pre-Tribulation rapture? *Just take us home now, Lord, the four of us, all together, before our lives become any more complicated.*

"Lord, haste the day when my faith shall be sight."

When it comes to the all-too-quickly growing-up of our girls, I long for a new world, where time fries. Perhaps this rapture craving is not just wishful thinking; it may signify more simmering below the surface than I care to admit. I might need the unsinged skin of Shadrach, Meshach, and Abednego to rub off on my shamefully timid faith.

Are the bushes around my half-life also starting to cover up my confidence and influence?

Maybe lamps are not the only thing in need of trimming!

A Pre-Tribulation rapture is not only a good way to not only avoid going through the teenage years with my girls but also to exempt us from being mentioned in the playbill of pathos and drama on Earth's stage as the End Times' curtain closes. I have never been able to foster genuine excitement at all for the prophetic broken seals, red moons, blood, and annihilation characteristic of the planet's twilight years. I know the "Patmos Exile" was all excited when he frantically wrote down his vision, but I am not. I feel like the disciples after Jesus had launched into that macabre analogy of "eating his flesh and drinking his blood." Long before horror movies, his speech severely thinned out the crowd who hurriedly exited to the theater lobby, waiting for the "Count the Cost" movie to be over. Jesus then turned to his Dynamic Dozen to check on their squeamishness, and they shrugged their shoulders and admitted to the Master that "there was nowhere else to go!" They were the fortunate ones in on holy truth, rendering all other diversions and detours a pack of lies—whether they liked it or not!

The only enticing aspect of the final curtain call that I can see is the comeuppance of the wicked. They are going to be eating, drinking, and making merry when "poverty will come like a bandit and scarcity like an armed man." Just like in the pre-wash days of Noah. As usual, I am reminded of a synopsis I presented to my 5th-graders some weeks back. I had intentionally left my hair wet from my Sunday-morning shower, and walked into our 10 x 12 Sunday school room wearing a yellow "slicker" raincoat. As soon as Sean, Leonard, Alex, and Robert were seated, I opened my umbrella, *indoors,* and, like a scroll, I unrolled a blueprint of a boat I had drawn the night before. I had imitated as best as I could the inimitable style of a draftsman using the typical chalky blue lead. I recited from the following that was taped inside of the blueprint:

> "There has been constant foot traffic due to spectator slowing for the past 100 years because a large cypress wood barge is being erected in the backyard of the Noah home. The 'My Three Sons' media frenzy continues each evening as the paparazzi attempt to nab an interview with Mr. and Mrs. Noah and their children. Usually, the family is caught off-guard on-camera with their hands dripping with pitch and their tunics covered in sweat

as some intrepid reporter, hungry for a scoop, seeks an interview. The family graciously cooperates with every photo op and press conference, and takes full advantage of the notoriety by passing out tracts detailing a future increase in moisture. Ararat-On-Line has created a wet-site called 'The Unsinkable Folly Clown,' where you can log on for the latest on the interminable boat-building. When the family finally climbs into their invention, the crowd roars with delight. Champagne bottles are broken over the boat as it just sits there on its 'maiden voyage.' The laughter dies down only when someone feels something wet on their head. Against all hope, all those who formerly logged on are now on logs."

"Open your Bibles, boys, to Genesis, Chapter Six."

The eating, drinking, and merry-making population of the Earth are going to get the shock of their lives when Jesus crashes the party. Non-believers are going to feel the same way I did one fateful Christmas morning. I was much older than appropriate, perhaps, but I had distinctly heard noises throughout the night on Christmas Eve emanating from our living room. I heard footsteps, bells, and packages rustling. Because my fertile imagination had frequently interrupted my eventual sleep, I woke up much later than intended on Christmas morning. I found my father, mother, and Owen sitting at the kitchen table, waiting for me. I could not keep quiet about the astounding events of the previous night. "Guess what? I heard him! I actually heard Santa Claus! Elves, too, possibly! They were making so much noise! I heard packages and—" Just then, Owen cruelly popped my childhood bubble: "Oh, come off it, Ian! Don't you know by now that there is no such thing as Santa Claus?" The look on his face told me that he was telling the truth, albeit insensitively. I was devastated.

Imagine the *reverse* devastation when the preoccupied world finds out that who *they* thought was mere myth, fable, or religious crutch, is, in fact, *real*! And, according to that famous Philippian letter, the first words out of Jolly Old St. Nick of Time will be "On your knees!"

As for me, I hesitate to think of my first physical encounter with Christ. Will He defer to His talent parable with that classic, sought-after approbation, "Well done, good and faithful servant"? After all that we have been through together, that sounds so austere and distant. Although the polarized hierarchical positions are biblically correct, it still feels a bit like an impersonal pat on the head from monarch to minion, or a chummy slap on the back from sovereign to slave, the suzerain deigning to barely recognize a long-term, loyal vassal.

With all due respect (and at the risk of trivializing what may lie ahead), I can create much more eternal anticipation for myself by picturing a scene not specifically found in the Bible. My first conscious moments on the "other side" find me standing in front of a '50s diner with a gold neon sign blinking "Messianic Malt Shop." I walk through the glass double doors and look around. The jukebox is playing a Rock 'n Roll version of "Blessed Assurance." At a long red booth in the corner of the diner, around a chrome-rimmed Formica table, sits Jesus and a bunch of His friends. "Hey, Ian—come on over!" Jesus says excitedly as He waves for me to come. I walk over and kneel in front of Him, placing the crown that has mysteriously appeared on my head on the glassy sea of the black-and-white square-tiled floor.

"Ian," speaks my Savior, with a beaming smile as He gently grabs my arm to help me up, "there are some people here who have been dying to meet you!" The other occupants of the crowded booth all laugh courteously at the well-worn joke. I stand up to see that Jesus' friends are actually all of *my* family and friends who have gone on before me. Jesus then tells the group, "Slide over and make room for my pal Ian. We have lots to talk about. Ian, you want a 7-Up or something? It's on me!"

Now *that* makes me want to reiterate the parting shot of Holy Scripture,

"Come Lord Jesus, make it so!"

In the meantime, I will do my part to hurry along the coming Kingdom as described by C.S. Lewis: "Enemy-occupied territory—that is what the world is. Christianity is the story of how the rightful King has landed in disguise, and is calling us all to take part in a great campaign of sabotage."

And then, heads are gonna roll!

THE END

About the Author

B rad Brown graduated with high honors with a Master's degree in Theology from Talbot School of Theology in La Mirada, California. He also graduated cum laude from Biola University with a degree in Speech Communication and a minor degree in Biblical Studies and Theology. He was voted the Most Outstanding Student of the Speech Communication Department for 1981–1982. *This Is The Church...* is followed by *Rightly Dividing?*, *Upon This Rock.*, and *Raised!*—the completed four "seasons" of Our Father's Evangelical Church.

Brad lives with his wife Cindy in Franktown, Colorado.